"Noreen has written a heart-hugging book about God's incredible grace intercepting those seeking abortion. Women no longer need to suffer in silence. There is hope and healing in God's love, acceptance, and forgiveness."

PAM VREDEVELT

AUTHOR OF *ANGEL BEHIND THE ROCKING CHAIR* AND *EMPTY ARMS*

"*My Unknown Child* is a welcome light at the end of abortion's long, dark tunnel. Noreen's profound honesty about her own abortion experience will touch you deeply. Share in her story as she strips away deception and offers hope and healing to any woman who is contemplating or has suffered from an abortion."

DAVID AND SANDE SUNDE

FAMILYLIFE COFOUNDERS

CAMPUS CRUSADE STAFF

"In the marketplace of ideas, women are sold the lie that abortion is simply a choice. But rarely are they told about the consequences. Noreen Riols takes us on her heartbreaking journey of pain and grief and, ultimately, healing. *My Unknown Child* personalizes the issue that not only is tearing this country apart but is breaking the hearts of women. Read Noreen's story and learn of the only way those hearts are put back together."

JANET PARSHALL

NATIONALLY SYNDICATED TALK RADIO HOST

"THIS BOOK WILL MOVE YOU TO THE DEPTHS OF YOUR BEING."

FLOODTIDE MAGAZINE

"Few people who have had an abortion have the courage or ability to express the long, terrible effects that this has had on them as individuals; Noreen Riols writes sensitively and movingly. This book should be widely read."

ANNE TOWNSEND

WRITER, GYNACOLOGIST

my
unknown
child

noreen riols

Multnomah®Publishers *Sisters, Oregon*

MY UNKNOWN CHILD
published by Multnomah Publishers, Inc.

© 1999 by Noreen Riols
International Standard Book Number: 1–57673–466–8

Cover photo of child by Marc Carter/Tony Stone Images
Cover photo of woman by Stephen Gardner
Design by Kirk DouPonce

Scripture quotations are from *The Holy Bible,* King James Version (KJV)
Also quoted:
The Good News Bible: The Bible in Today's English Version (TEV) © 1976 by
American Bible Society

The Holy Bible, New International Version (NIV)
© 1973, 1984 by International Bible Society,
used by permission of Zondervan Publishing House

Multnomah is a trademark of Multnomah Publishers, Inc., and is registered in the
U.S. Patent and Trademark Office.
The colophon is a trademark of Multnomah Publishers, Inc.

Printed in the United States of America

For information:
Multnomah Publishers, Inc. • Post Office Box 1720 • Sisters, Oregon 97759

Library of Congress Cataloging-in-Publication Data:
Riols, Noreen.
My Unknown Child/Noreen Riols.
         p.   cm.
ISBN 1–57673–466–8
1. Abortion—France—Psychological aspects. 2. Abortion—
Religious aspects—Christianity. 3. Pregnant women—France—
Psychology. I. Title
HQ767.F7R56   1999
363.46—dc21   99–12862
                                                                    CIP
99 00 01 02 03 04 05 — 10 9 8 7 6 5 4 3 2 1

preface

Since this book was first published in Europe, a whole new world has been opened up to me—a world of suffering, often hidden suffering. Women who have read the book have written or come to see me because having experienced the same trauma following an abortion, they identified with what I had gone through. It is a trauma that they have not dared to reveal through fear of condemnation or judgment on the part of others. An abortion is a death without mourning, without a funeral, and without dignity.

I have come to realize that no woman escapes the pain. The guilt and depression may not be instantaneous, as it was in my case. It may not even occur within the first few months or even years after an abortion. But in the end it catches up with the mother, and she realizes what she has done. She has signed the death warrant of her own child. It doesn't help that she did so following good, loving, and professional advice because she knows that the final decision was hers. There is no one she can blame. Had she not signed that paper authorizing the abortion, no one could have torn her growing baby from her body.

What has surprised and appalled me on the many occasions I have been asked to speak on the subject, not only in England but also in Continental Europe, is the ignorance of the general public about what actually happens in an abortion. I understand, because I was ignorant myself. I believed it was a clot of blood or a mass of jelly that was to be removed from my uterus. Had the doctors told me the truth—that they would be obliged to massacre a miniature human being, tearing it limb from limb, my baby, who already loved me, who was happy when I was happy, who reacted at the sound of my voice—I could never have agreed to an abortion.

And I would today have a thirty-year-old son or daughter.

Doctors are busy people. But it would take much less time to inform a woman considering an abortion about what will actually happen and the likely repercussions than it would to perform the operation or counsel her afterwards.

I am also shocked by what is taught, or not taught, in schools. No one appears to tell our young people the stark truth. They have been brought up with legalized abortion as a fact of life. For them it is a right, their right.

After speaking to a teenage group only a few months ago, one boy of sixteen came up to me, shattered by what he had heard. "That's not what we learn in school," he said. "We're encouraged to use condoms and are told if our girlfriend becomes pregnant, it's not a problem, she can have an abortion! Everybody's doing it."

I was able to reply that even if every one of his classmates was "doing it," which I doubted, there were still some who weren't. He wasn't obliged to join the mob. The choice was his. But I understood his feelings. How hard it is not to be "with it," not be part of the group. And for those who hesitate, it makes the decision to abort easier if they can believe, as he did, that "everybody's doing it." It somehow reinforces the "right."

My heart bleeds for our young people. What terrible pressures we are putting on them with all this freedom of choice. But a fetus isn't a choice—it's a human baby. What they are not being told is that freedom has a price tag, a price many of us spend the rest of our lives repaying.

In an abortion there are always two victims: the baby who dies, but also the mother, who has to live the rest of her life with her guilt and remorse. When my baby died, something died in me also, and I am sure I am not alone in this. The terrible thing is that an abortion is irrevocable. All the tears in the world won't bring the baby back. Jesus can heal and forgive us, and he will if we ask him. But the consequences of an abortion remain. We have to live with the memory of our unknown child, the baby who might have been.

Is this *really* the legacy we want to hand on to our children and our grandchildren growing up in the world of today?

Marly-le-roi, 1999

one

When I heard the soft shuffle of Yves's bunny rabbit slippers and saw him appear round the bend of the stairs, the belt of his yellow bathrobe trailing behind him, it was the last straw.

It had been an exhausting day, both physically and mentally. In fact, it had been an exhausting week. Knowing that Yves was safely tucked up in bed and supposedly sound asleep had been one less worry to cope with. But now here he was, wide awake, his china blue eyes staring inquiringly at the preparations for departure strewn around the hall.

Jacques, my husband, walked in through the front door at that moment, smiled at his four-year-old son and ruffled his hair.

"I won't have time for dinner," he called over his shoulder as he ran up the stairs two at a time. "If you're ready, we'd better be off."

Yves stopped dead in his tracks.

"Where are you going?" he inquired belligerently.

I dropped to one knee and cuddled him in my arms.

"I won't be away for long, darling," I murmured into the silky smoothness of his soft, fair hair. "Daddy will be here, and Bee and your brothers."

An earsplitting wail came from the drawing room where ten-year-old Bee was lying full length on the sofa trying to play the Tongan nose flute, which an obviously hard-of-hearing friend had given her for Christmas.

"Don't worry," I ended lamely, my words punctuated by a piercing crescendo. "I'll bring you back a present."

"But where are you going?" Yves demanded, drawing away from me and looking intently into my face, his eyes wide and puzzled.

"I've got to go away for a few days," I stammered, "to England."

His face lit up.

"To see Grannie and Grandpa?" he exclaimed. "I'm coming with you!"

And he turned toward the stairs, pulling off his bathrobe as he went.

"Yves," I called helplessly, catching him on the bottom step. "Darling, you can't come with me."

"Why not?" he cried, turning around, his eyes now more puzzled than ever.

I was on the verge of tears.

"You stay and help look after Christopher," I stumbled over the words, thinking of the chubby baby peacefully sleeping in his crib upstairs. "He'd be lonely without you to play with…and I won't be away long."

Yves stared at me long and hard, and his bottom lip started to quiver.

"Christopher's only a *baby*," he pouted. "He can come another time."

My tears were now threatening to overflow and spoil any effect of casualness I had hoped to produce, but mercifully, Olivier came to my rescue.

"Come on, Yves," his elder brother said firmly, "I'll take you back to bed."

"I don't *want* to go back to bed," Yves wailed and began to cry. "I want to go to England with Mummie."

"You can't go to England with Mummie, and that's that," said Olivier firmly, picking him up in his arms.

Yves cried and wriggled, but his brother had him in an iron grip.

My husband came clattering back down the stairs and winced at the combined racket of Yves and the nose flute.

"Does she have to blow that thing so hard?" he inquired.

"I don't think she blows it," I replied absently, "rather sucks."

Then I stopped and almost laughed at the absurdity of our conversation at such a fraught moment. But laughter had been far from my lips during the past few months.

"What's wrong, Yves?" Jacques inquired, totally

unaware of the previous conversation. "Had a bad dream?"

"No," wailed Yves, struggling to go to his father. "I want to come to England with you and Mummie."

"*I'm* not going," Jacques said, taking the bewildered little boy in his arms, "only Mummie. And she won't be away long."

"Listen," he went on, holding Yves away from him and staring into his tear-stained face, "we'll have a lot of fun together. How would you like to go on a boat on the lake, like we did when Mummie was in the hospital with Christopher? We could buy popcorn and take bread to feed the ducks, too."

Yves rubbed his chubby knuckles into his eyes and brightened up momentarily. Then, obviously weighing up in his little mind the tepid excitement of a boat on the lake compared to the alternative of going to see Grannie and Grandpa, started to cry again.

"No," he said, "I want to go to England."

I bit my lip and looked at my watch. Time was running short, yet I couldn't leave Yves in this state. Suddenly I felt like giving up the whole thing.

"I'm not going," I announced wearily, sitting down heavily on the oak settle.

Yves stared from one of us to the other and, seeing both his treats rapidly fading into the distance, surprisingly made no attempt to struggle when his eldest brother firmly moved him from his father's arms.

"Don't worry about him," Olivier said steadily, "he'll be all right as soon as you're gone. Now go," he ended sharply, "you've barely time to catch the train as it is."

Jacques came and took my arm.

"Don't forget…" I began rising hesitantly on my feet.

"Just *go*," said Olivier exasperatedly. "Everything will be all right. Stop worrying."

Bee appeared, that wretched nose flute dangling from her hand. It was a relief to have even temporary respite from its piercing wail. She skipped over to me, her skinny brown braids dancing up and down, and her dark, expressive eyes sparkling.

I bent to kiss her.

"Don't forget to bring me back lots of Smarties," she whispered, clinging to my neck.

"Come *on*," said Jacques, tugging me away from her grasp.

I looked helplessly at Yves still imprisoned in Olivier's arms, and as I caught his eyes, his lips quivered. Olivier had also noticed the warning sign.

"Let's go and wave them good-bye," he coaxed and, putting his little brother down, took hold of his hand and ran with him down the steps.

For Yves the excitement of being out in the street in his bathrobe after dark momentarily took away the implications of the reason for his being there. I turned round as the car sped up the hill to see him holding firmly on to

Olivier's hand as Bee waved her Tongan flute in farewell, and the tears, now released, began to flow freely down my face.

Jacques took his hand off the wheel and closed it over mine.

"Don't worry," he soothed. "They'll be all right…and it's not for long. You'll be back in a few days."

I nodded bleakly.

That was what we both thought at the time. But it didn't prove to be as simple as we had been led to believe.

After two weeks of anguish and procrastination, I had finally made the devastating decision to have the unplanned child I was carrying aborted. Knowing that I was English, my medical advisors, who had told me that another baby would cost me my sanity, had suggested I go to London where, according to them, "it was easy."

In 1967, abortion was strictly illegal in France and carried with it heavy sanctions, so only "back-street abortions" were available to those women who could not afford the luxury of a private clinic in Switzerland. There the operation was carried out with utmost discretion and secrecy…and at enormous expense. The phrase "She's gone to Switzerland for a few days" often carried sinister undertones—and didn't always mean for a skiing weekend.

Jacques and I had both been shocked by the apparent flippancy of this remark, which we heard from time to time, and more so now because we were ourselves faced with the same decision, and we didn't like it at all. But in sizing up the grim alternative, the threat to my mental health that the psychiatrists had predicted, we felt helpless and incapable of swimming against the tide.

At least I did. I know Jacques would have supported me had I decided to take the chance and have the baby, but the terrible postnatal depression I had suffered with Christopher's birth had left me incapable of even thinking straight, let alone making a decision. The months of hospitalization in a psychiatric clinic had left me weak and feeling utterly hopeless. And all this, added to the guilt that the decision had placed upon me, had taken its toll. The drugs had drained me dry: I was limp and exhausted, and felt unable to go on.

Jacques and I had concluded that it would be less traumatic for me to go back to the large London hospital where I had trained as a nurse years before. When I telephoned to ask for their advice they had been kind and sympathetic and arranged for me to see a well-known consultant, but they had also asked for letters and case histories from the gynecologist and psychiatrists who had treated me both before Christopher's birth and during my postnatal depression and subsequent breakdown. Now the papers were all in order, and I was to see this specialist in London on the following day.

As the car raced through the quiet streets and on to the Gare du Nord, where the night ferry would soon be snorting its way out of the grimy station, I kept seeing in my mind Yves and Olivier standing in the street waving goodbye, and it was like history repeating itself.

"Do you remember when you took me to the hospital to have Christopher?" I asked Jacques.

"Will I ever forget it?" He smiled. "The shortest night of my life."

My husband had had a business dinner that evening and had rolled gratefully into bed at one o'clock only to be up and on his way to the hospital half an hour later. And once again Olivier had come to the rescue.

At fifteen, he was not always easy, but we knew that in a crisis we could rely on him. It had never occurred to us to awaken Herve, who, at fourteen, was much more easy going, but who would probably have promised to keep watch and then promptly fallen sound asleep again. Olivier had volunteered to move into our bed so that if one of the younger ones should come looking for us, they would not find it empty.

I had been grateful for his thoughtfulness. But as we were leaving, just like this evening, Yves had appeared on the scene and demanded to know where we were going and why he couldn't come with us. It was weird: I remembered so well stopping as I left the house and taking him in my arms and him clinging to me and Olivier saying, just as he had tonight after finally prizing Yves from me, "For goodness' sake—go!"

Olivier had understood the urgency of the situation then. It had been obvious. But now? We hadn't told the children why I was going, merely that I had to have some tests done in the hospital and, strangely enough, they had accepted our explanation without question. But what had they really thought? I don't think Herve and Bee had thought anything, but Olivier? Had he, with that almost uncanny perception of his, guessed the reason for my journey? Was that why he had been so adamant with Yves and had managed to quieten him down? And I wondered whether in the years to come if I would ever have the courage to tell the children what I had done. I shuddered at the thought.

"Has it struck you that the night Christopher was born was exactly like tonight?" I asked. "Yves coming down just as we were leaving, and he and Olivier standing outside the house as we left? Only then it was a happy occasion.... Now it's the reverse."

And as we drove through the Bois de Boulogne, where I had spent so many happy afternoons with Bee in her preschool days while she skipped or ran delightedly with her hoop, I relapsed into a brooding silence.

The car turned onto Victor Hugo Avenue, where Jacques was born and had lived all his life till we moved out to Marly village on the outskirts of Paris the summer after his mother had died from a sudden heart attack.

Passing the block of flats where his father still lived, where we had spent the first years of our marriage, I looked up and remembered with gratitude my mother-in-law's kindness to me, her gentleness, her complete acceptance of me—a foreigner—who had married her only son. I knew that had she been alive, I would have left with an easier conscience. She would have come quietly down the two flights of stairs separating our apartments and comforted Yves, gently urged Bee to go to bed, and soothed any upsets or tensions my hurried departure provoked.

Yves had been born the year after she died. I still regretted that she had never known this sensitive blond child, and he had not known her. She would have been such a haven for him in moments of stress.

The words that the Protestant pastor had pronounced at her funeral because he said they so typified her, came to my mind: "Peace I leave with you, my peace I give you, not as the world gives do I give to you." How right he had been. Jacques' mother had been such a serene, loving person, one who had an aura of tranquillity about her and who spread peace wherever she went.

We approached the ghostly white contours of the Arc de Triomphe at the far end of the avenue. A flag furled and unfurled beneath it in a misty haze as the evening breeze swirled the last of the leaves around the trees. I turned and looked at my husband, realizing that he had inherited that peace from his mother, and with a sigh, I wondered how I, too, could acquire it. Mistaking my sigh for distress, Jacques once again took his hand from the wheel and placed it over mine as we drove in silence, the minutes speeding on as the lights of Paris flashed past us.

We arrived at the Gare du Nord with eight minutes to spare and, hurrying onto the platform, found the sleeping car attendant waiting for last-minute arrivals.

two

I have always loved trains, right from my earliest childhood, which often found us going off with buckets and spades and shrimping nets to what so often proved to be rainy holidays at the seaside.

But I especially love the excitement of large railway stations at night. The noise, the bustle, so different from the daytime clamor, the very smell has always thrilled me. And the night ferry that no longer speeds, as such, between London and Paris, held a particular fascination for me.

The warm narrow coziness of the small compartment-turned-bedroom. The smell of leather and mahogany and the minute washbasin set in a corner with an oblong mirror above, all spelled adventure, romance, travel. The thrill of pulling up the blind as the train ground slowly away from the platform and glimpsing other trains panting, ready to leave for Moscow, Kraków, Budapest, Amsterdam, Stockholm. All those intriguing capitals! Then hearing the comforting creak as I climbed into my bunk to be lulled to sleep by the clickety-clack of the wheels rolling rhythmi-cally over the rails.

The white-coated attendant took the ticket Jacques gave him. I handed over my passport, and we climbed aboard. I was lucky; there were very few people traveling and the upper bunk was empty—I had the compartment to myself.

As Jacques put down my suitcase, there was a warning whistle. Suddenly afraid, I looked at my husband and grabbed desperately at his coat lapel, clinging to him, unwilling to let him go and be left alone with this dreadful secret.

Jacques put his arms around me and held me close. I felt a choking sob rise in my throat. But the moment was too fraught for words or even for tears. The whistle sounded again, ominous. Pressing his face quickly against mine, planting a swift brotherly kiss on my cold cheek, Jacques gently released my hands, and as the engine hummed and the train jerked, he jumped down onto the bleak, dimly lit platform. As I watched miserably through the window, we began to move slowly from the station, past the women pushing wheelbarrows loaded with blankets and pillows, past the porters, past the signs, until my husband was just a small figure standing in the distance, and the train was already racing away into the black winter night.

I lay there in the darkness, the small blue light above the door casting a ghostlike aura into the compartment.

My mind refused to let me sleep. The exhaustion and tension of the last few days rolled my taut nerves into a tight ball. Even the gentle swaying of the train and the regular lullaby of the steel wheels only served to remind me of where I was going...and why.

My trips to England had always been such happy occasions before, and as I lay in the eerie darkness, I remembered how the year before I had traveled this same route with Yves in the upper bunk and Christopher lying in an infant carrier on the floor at my side. He had been only four months old at the time, and instead of being rocked to sleep by the rhythm of the train, he had been jerked into wakefulness. When I had leaned out of my bunk to look at him, his deep violet-blue eyes had returned my stare.

A few years earlier it had been Bee in the upper bunk and Yves in an infant carrier on the floor. But this time I was alone, and I would never again travel with a baby on the floor beside me. I turned impatiently in the tightly tucked-in sheets, seeking sleep, finding none, and tried to push the futile thoughts from my mind. What was the point in going endlessly back over the same question? I had made my decision. . .or at least I thought I had.

But as I lay there, I realized that other people had made the decision for me.

The psychiatrists and gynecologist had been adamant that another baby would put me in a mental home for the rest of my life. Even our vicar, whom I had telephoned in desperation, had agreed with them. He was a kindly, older man with an almost grown-up family, and he and his wife had visited me in the psychiatric clinic. He knew my history, so I felt free to talk to him and hoped that perhaps he would be able to give something more than just "clinical" advice. When he came round immediately in answer to my call, he had been very understanding, but he had also been very firm.

"If it were my wife in your position," he had said gently, holding my hand as the never-ending tears streamed down my face, "knowing what you've gone through, I wouldn't hesitate. You must think of the other five children. What is going to happen to them if you are locked away for the rest of your life?"

I didn't know. But I remembered wondering miserably whether they wouldn't all be better off without me. I hadn't been much use to them in the last few months.

I think the vicar read my thoughts.

"You have no choice," he said quietly.

And, bleakly, I had agreed with him.

Only Jacques had understood and known my deep longing for another child. But finally fatigue and that overwhelming, black, postnatal depression that had inexplicably descended upon me three days after the joy of Christopher's birth and was still clutching me in its lethal fangs, added to the pressure of outside advice, had brought me to where I was now—traveling miserably through the night to put an end to the new life that was growing inside me.

Jacques' words to me that evening after the vicar's visit, as I agonized over what he had said, came back to me. "If you really want to go through with this, then go ahead and have the baby—we'll manage somehow."

Knowing him, I was sure he would have managed. But what would the "somehow" have been? A series of nannies and housekeepers to look after the children? The bewilderment for them of a mother who had finally vanished forever without explanation or mourning or the finality and dignity of a funeral, only whispers behind closed doors, the inevitable revelation, and the stigma of learning that she was a long-term patient in a mental home?

I knew I couldn't be responsible for inflicting that scar on their lives.

As the train raced through the night, I lay there endlessly going over the events of the past years, remembering my first meeting with Jacques in postwar London and our linking up again in Paris in the fifties and the love and kindness of Jacques' family when I married him and became stepmother to Olivier, Herve, and Bee.

In spite of my tangled emotions, I did sleep, awakened as I always was to the shouts of the French seamen as they guided the train onto the boat at Dunkerque. Then the gentle swaying movement as we crossed the Channel taking me back to England caused me to drift off to sleep once again, to be roused by English voices as the train arrived at

Dover and stood panting in the station.

These were the sounds I knew and loved and looked forward to. To me, no airport, no airplane trip could ever replace the thrill I felt at these different noises coming in the night and the ultimate excitement of pulling up the window shade as the train started on its final journey and watching the orchards and green fields of Kent speed past the windows.

As we approached the outskirts of London there was a tap on the door, and the attendant came in carrying a steaming cup of tea and my passport.

"Arriving in Victoria in half an hour, madam," he announced and withdrew.

I sipped my tea thoughtfully, then slowly got up and prepared to face this day that was to be such a momentous one for me. The train began to slow down, and I heard the familiar sounds of that great London station that had welcomed me and seen me off so many times in the past few years.

There was a light drizzle falling as I walked under the archway and out into the street, and London looked cold and gray and wintry. I stopped at a flower stall and bought a large bunch of multicolored blooms before hailing a taxi and giving an address in Chelsea.

When I had decided to come to London, I had no idea where I was going to stay.

My parents lived in Essex, which was hardly practical,

and anyway, not knowing how they would react, I didn't want to involve them in this problem. They were wonderful grandparents and would have been delighted to learn that another baby was on the way. Although I knew that knowing the truth they would not condemn me but just go on loving me, I didn't want to cause them pain.

The thought of staying in a hotel alone in my present neurotic state was out of the question. It just happened (and as I was later to discover when I became a committed Christian that many events in our lives appear to "just happen") that a good friend who knew of my plight suggested I go to stay with her mother's cousin who lived alone and, according to her, would be delighted to put me up. I wasn't so sure she would be, but when Charlotte called and said, "I telephoned Mary, and she's looking forward to meeting you," I took the invitation at face value.

But now that I had arrived, I began to have qualms and to wonder just how right I had been to push myself onto someone I had never even met. However, I had said I would go along to breakfast straight from the train, so I decided to go anyway and take it from there.

As the taxi stopped in that quiet Chelsea square in front of a tall, narrow house, the door opened and Mary appeared on the step.

"Welcome." She smiled. "Charlotte told me you'd be arriving about this time, and I've been looking out of the window, waiting for the taxi to pull up."

She opened the door wide and held out her hand for my suitcase. It was like coming home.

Mary was small and dainty and must have been well over sixty. But her step was that of a young girl. As she led me through the narrow hall, a warm, comforting smell of coffee and toast rose to greet me.

"I'll take you to your room," she said, climbing the stairs in front of me. "My other guest only left yesterday, but it's all ready and made up for you."

I began to protest, feeling what an imposition it was to come tumbling in upon a total stranger like this. But Mary turned around and smiled.

"Don't worry," she said. "I love having people to stay." And she opened the door of a small pretty room with rose chintz curtains at the window.

Although the drizzle outside had now turned to a steady downpour, the room was warm and cozy and inviting and I immediately felt at home.

"I'll leave you," Mary said. "I think there's everything you need."

She waved her hand in the direction of the sink and the soft, fluffy pink towels hanging on a rail beside it.

"If not, you've only to shout. I'll be in the kitchen putting the finishing touches on breakfast. Come down when you're ready."

She picked up my bouquet from the small bedside table where she had placed it.

"How sweet of you to bring me these flowers," she murmured, burying her nose in the sodden blooms. She looked at me over the top of them and smiled. "Don't worry," she went on softly, "Charlotte told me why you're here. Just make this your home for as long as you need to." And closing the door behind her, she tripped lightly back down the stairs.

I walked over to the window and stood looking down on the tiny paved garden below, the tears once again rising. I began to wonder if there would ever again be a time in my life when I was not constantly awash with tears. The last year or so had seemed like the great flood, as far as I was concerned.

Sitting down on the flowered bedspread, I gazed gratefully at the closed door, Mary's parting words echoing through my head: *Don't worry, Charlotte told me why you're here.*

So she knew—the utter relief. And she didn't appear to condemn. I didn't have to pretend I was here for tests or pretend anything, in fact. It was all out in the open, and at last I could relax.

three

The rain had stopped when I left the house and began to walk through the damp, gray London streets toward the hospital.

It was a fair distance, and normally I would have taken a bus. But that afternoon I wanted to recapture old memories. Or so I thought. Perhaps in my subconscious mind I just wanted to put off the moment of truth, the time when the final, irrevocable decision would have to be made.

It had been many years since I finished my training, and I wondered what it would feel like to be back. It occurred to me that perhaps it would have been better to have chosen somewhere neutral, a hospital I had never entered before. But as I crossed under the heavy portal and smelled the familiar smells, saw the endless procession of white-coated doctors and residents and the nurses in their starched aprons and little lace caps walking purposefully down the main corridor, I again had that same feeling of warmth and security and of coming home that I had experienced upon entering Mary's guest room.

The layout of the hospital had changed since my time. Not knowing quite where to go, I turned into a side corridor leading to what, in my day, had been the matron's office—the spot we all rushed to when coming on and off duty to collect our mail. It hadn't changed. There was still a crowd of nurses in striped dresses and stiff collars clustered around the alphabetical slots, their frilly caps bobbing up and down as they searched the cubbyholes for letters.

I stood for a moment, my mind spinning back down the years to when I had been a carefree probationer rushing off duty for the four-hour afternoon break, remembering the fun of communal living and, as we mercifully do, forgetting the rigid rules, the tiredness and the plain hard slog of nursing in a large London hospital in those lean days just after the end of the war.

There was a tap on my shoulder and a voice said, "It's Nurse Baxter, isn't it?"

I spun around to face one of the sisters whom I had so dreaded in those far-off days. She was smiling and seemed genuinely pleased to see me.

I smiled back, a little diffidently, suddenly afraid that she would ask why I was there, and I would see the condemnation in her eyes—those same eyes that had so often been steely when we faced each other after I had yet again done something that fell short of her, what were to me, impossibly high standards. I had been a particularly tiresome thorn in her side when she was night sister, always managing to do the wrong things and constantly being reprimanded for mistakes I'd made, which in my eyes seemed trivial but in hers took on enormous proportions.

"How nice to see you," she said, and I had the feeling she meant it. "You haven't been to any of the fellowship meetings…but I heard you were living abroad now."

"Yes," I replied, "in Paris."

"How lovely," she went on, and raised her eyebrows inquiringly.

"I've come to see Professor Ponting," I said, in answer to her unspoken question.

"As a matter of fact," I blurted out, looking at my watch, "my appointment's in five minutes. But everything's changed so I panicked and turned into the only corridor that was familiar to me."

We both laughed.

"Of course. When you were in training we were still living with bomb damage." She smiled and took my arm, leading me back to the main corridor.

I reeled slightly at this human touch, for I hadn't thought of her as "human" at all. In fact, we had nicknamed her "the dragon." Yet, looking at her now, her face showing the lines of advancing years, I saw deep compassion mirrored in her wide, gray eyes, and I thought what a pretty woman she must have been once. I'd only been conscious of her seemingly impossible standards and the strict discipline she enforced and had squirmed under the firm, unyielding yoke. Now, with hindsight, I saw her in a different light and felt an overwhelming gratitude for the way she had instilled in all of us the principles she lived by.

I suddenly felt I wanted to make up to her for the hard feelings I'd had, we'd all had. But in those few moments, I didn't know how.

She released my arm and pointed to the end of the long, wide corridor.

"Go right to the end and down the staircase, where the emergency room used to be when you were in training, and you'll see the department signposted. Third door on the right for Professor Ponting's appointments. Good luck." And she smiled again.

Perhaps she understood the reason for my being here. I wanted to shake her hand, even to affectionately peck her cheek as the French do so spontaneously. But I wondered whether it would embarrass her, whether she would understand. The English of my generation and even more so of hers, seemed so afraid of physical contact in public. But I felt that having glimpsed that other side of her, the caring, compassionate side, I couldn't let her go like that. I thought she must be nearing retirement age, and perhaps I would never see her again.

"I came back here to the hospital," I faltered, "because…because I know it inside out, and I know its worth and…now that I've met you again after all these years I'd like to say thank you for all that you taught me. I don't think I appreciated it at the time. But I realize now the devotion of you sisters, and how difficult we must sometimes have made your lives."

She looked at me in surprise and her eyes clouded. Were thanks so rare to her? Then she smiled.

"Don't think we didn't understand," she ended. "I was a probationer once, you know...before the war. And it's not always easy to be strict and insist on standards...to be unpopular, in fact. But thank you for telling me it was worth it."

Quickly turning on her heels, she disappeared back into the corridor where we had bumped into each other. A small erect figure, her impeccable white apron creaking with starch, the tall, white cap with the little bow under the chin sitting stiff and uncompromising on her graying bun.

Professor Ponting was tall, white-haired and distinguished. I liked him immediately and felt less nervous than expected as I sat in front of his desk while he looked through the sheath of reports I had brought—letters from my gynecologist and from the two psychiatrists who had treated me after my breakdown and the results of endless tests.

Then he looked up and smiled. "I see you've been through a difficult time," he said quietly.

I smiled back weakly. "It hasn't been easy," I replied,

"for anyone…for my family as much as for me."

He nodded sympathetically. "I can well imagine," was his only comment.

The interview was much easier than I had expected. The professor was kind and understanding but, contrary to what I had anticipated, he didn't say, as the psychiatrists in Paris had led me to believe, "Come in tomorrow and you'll be home by the weekend."

He looked at me over the rim of his half-moon spectacles and gave me an engaging smile.

"I'd like you to see two of my colleagues," he announced, "before we make a decision."

I was shattered, thinking that the decision rested on him alone. And I told him so.

"You're quite right," he answered. "The decision of whether to *operate* is mine. But we are talking about the suppression of a human life. I don't wish to take such a step without being absolutely sure that it is the right one. But the decision as to whether, once I've decided, I *do* operate, is yours and yours alone. And in that decision I have absolutely no say. I can only advise."

The professor gathered his papers together and stood up. His deep blue eyes seemed to bore right through me and I avoided his gaze. I wondered what I would do if he decided not to operate. And finally I realized that in the end the decision was mine, however much I tried to shuffle the responsibility onto someone else.

"Dr. Wing will be here tomorrow," I heard him saying. "I'm afraid I don't know his schedule, so perhaps you could telephone around nine in the morning and make an appointment to see him."

The name *Dr. Wing* didn't ring a bell, and at that moment, I felt drained and exhausted, incapable of thinking. The sleepless night, the tense few days before my departure and now, instead of going into the hospital and getting it over with, I saw stretching before me an endless succession of white coats and interviews—repeating my case history until it seemed to me that I was back once again in that closed tunnel through which I had been groping all these months. And there was *still* no way out.

I got unsteadily to my feet, and the professor motioned to the nurse who had just come through the door with the next file.

"I'm sure Mrs. Riols would like a cup of tea," he said. "She's coming back tomorrow to see Dr. Wing."

I went to shake his hand. Then I remembered I was in England and only a smile and a nod were necessary.

The nurse held open the door. As I went through, I told her I was in a hurry and not to bother about the tea. She nodded and returned to her desk. Walking back into the brightly lit corridor, I remembered the endless cups of tea, the British panacea for all ills, that I had made for upset visitors and frightened patients during my years of training. And it brought a comforting spread of warmth through me as once again my mind traveled back through the years.

Dr. Wing was unable to see me until late the following afternoon. As I walked into the consulting room, he rose and smiled and his face seemed vaguely familiar. Where had I seen him before? He looked at me strangely too, as though he were asking himself the same question. Motioning for me to sit in front of his desk, he sat down and started thumbing through my papers.

"I see you're one of us," he said, looking up.

"Yes," I replied, my mind still puzzling as to where I could have met him. "But a long time ago."

"From all accounts, at about the same time as I was a resident," he volunteered, and then suddenly his face clicked into position, a younger face, without the creases on his forehead or the lines around his eyes. The thinning brown hair became a thick, unruly mass, and I remembered my last New Year's Eve ball at the hospital when he had been one of our party, and the times when I had been in charge of a ward on night duty in my last year and had called him out to a patient. I could still see him arriving in the dimly lit ward, his hair disheveled and his stethoscope sticking out of his short, white jacket pocket, blinking off sleep as he hurried to the bedside. And then the cup of cocoa and thick slice of bread and margarine one of us always prepared for him in the ward kitchen when the emergency was over and he was finally able to stagger back to his cot in the basement before the next call dragged him out.

The same click must have happened in his brain, for suddenly we both started to laugh as the memories flooded back.

"What a long time ago it all was," he remarked. "And now you live in Paris."

"Yes," I replied, "where the psychiatrists told me to come to London, 'where it's easy.'"

"That's what they all think," he answered dryly. "And it causes us endless problems."

His eyes dropped to my folder again. "I haven't spoken to Professor Ponting yet, but from what I gather, I think I would advise that we go ahead and terminate this pregnancy. But of course it's not a decision I can make on my own. We are a team of three, and the professor has the final word."

"When do you think you'll be able to speak to him?" I murmured.

"Not until Friday," he said apologetically. "He's attending an important conference on this very subject and won't be back until tomorrow night."

My heart sank, and I gasped.

He looked up at me. "Are you worrying about the time factor?" he inquired. "It's not quite three months; I don't think there's a problem there."

"No," I mumbled, "it's not that. It's just the waiting. It

took me long enough to make up my mind, and now that it's done, I'm afraid I want instant action."

"I understand," he said kindly, "but as it is, I'm afraid there's absolutely nothing I can do to help you."

"You have helped me," I smiled. "Just meeting you again and laughing has broken the horrible tension I've been living under these past weeks. It's helped me to get things in perspective and stop thinking I'm the center of the universe."

He stood up and laughed. "From what I remember, I don't think of you like that. But as you say, it's good to laugh. We don't seem to do it often enough these days."

He came round the desk and helped me on with my coat.

"I don't think there's any need for you to see Bob, the third member of our team. I can show him your case history and explain how things are, and if it's all right with the boss, he and I can make the decision. You've been grilled enough, and if our old friendship can spare you that, well, it's worth something."

I smiled gratefully at him. We hadn't been particular friends, just colleagues. But it was strange how these far-off links had become strong once the mother-link with the hospital had been broken and we had all scattered to live our various lives. And I realized that it couldn't be every day he had familiar faces from his time as a resident come to consult him.

"Would you mind making an appointment for Friday? I'll tell the nurse it's urgent and she has to fit you in. Where are you staying, by the way?"

"With friends in Chelsea," I replied mechanically.

"Good," he answered. "We can get in touch with you easily if necessary."

"Yes," I answered, my thoughts already far away.

We smiled at each other as I walked past him into the waiting room beyond.

It had been a gray, drizzly day. Dusk was creeping over the city as I walked out of the hospital. Night was falling, and London became alive with a thousand lights glittering on the river and in the still, damp air. The rain had left behind it a soft mist and the nearby lights seemed to be circled in gold as they shed their glow on the damp pavement. Big Ben struck the half hour, and people poured in a solid mass in and out of every underground station. I decided I couldn't face the crowded subway and stepped out swiftly to walk back to Chelsea.

Mary was waiting for me in her cozy first-floor drawing room, her hands busy with a piece of needlepoint. She smiled when I came in but didn't ask any questions, for which I was grateful.

"Dinner will be ready in about half an hour," she said. "Come and warm yourself by the fire. The damp outside is enough to freeze your bones."

She patted the sofa beside her as she leaned forward to

poke the fire into a spurt of flame.

I sat down and gazed at the sputtering logs, grateful not only for the warmth but for the security it offered. Leaping flames and cozy hearths were things that I remembered from my childhood. Rushing in from school on a frosty afternoon to sit before the blaze and toast bread on a long fork in the firelight. The scorching heat on my face, the crunch of butter-soaked toast and the shock of scalding tea as we sat cross-legged on the carpet having nothing but to enjoy the sensation of food and the comforting warmth of home and fire. Simple pleasures that seemed to have vanished from present-day life. From everyone's life.

We had a log fire at home in Marly, but the children had so many more distractions nowadays, more homework, more demands on their time, and the joy of just sitting, contemplating the blaze and thinking of nothing in particular seemed to be a luxury that was denied them.

I sighed, and Mary looked up inquiringly.

"I was thinking about the past," I said in explanation.

"We always think the past is perfect," she answered laconically, "and that only the present is bad."

"I suppose so," I replied. "But I was remembering the simple joys of a fire and nothing to do as a child but look at it."

Mary didn't reply immediately, then picking up her scissors, she snipped a piece of wool.

"For those who were lucky enough to have nothing to

do," she said dryly. "Let the past lie. The present does have its good points, and it is, after all, what you make of it."

I saw her point.

"You're right," I said, and knew that this was the moment to tell her the news she obviously wanted.

"It looks as if I've got to hang around for another week," I said tersely.

For a moment there was silence, then Mary laid aside her needlepoint and turned to me.

"Noreen," she said gently, "you know you're more than welcome to stay here, and I'd love to have you, but once the decision is made and you don't have to go rushing backward and forward to the hospital, don't you think it would be kinder to go see your parents?"

I looked up, startled.

"They're bound to find out you've been over," she went on. "People always do. And since you're going to be in England for longer than you expected, it would be awful for them if they heard from someone else. They'd feel you hadn't been able to trust them."

"Oh, it's not that," I protested.

Mary looked me straight in the eyes. "Then what is it?" she inquired.

I paused, not sure that I knew the answer myself.

"I don't want to hurt them," I burst out at last. "They're kind and loving and I know how much I mean to them."

I bit my lip, searching for words.

"I don't want them to be disappointed in me...or...to judge me, even if they never put it in so many words."

A log fell into the ashes, and a sudden flame sprang up and hissed in the silence.

"I'm only an old maid," Mary said at last. "I've never had children and can only imagine what I'd feel. But if I had a daughter and she hadn't felt she could trust me in a situation as important as this one, I know I'd be terribly hurt. After all, it's not only your child that is under sentence, it's also their grandchild."

I sat for a moment, stunned.

Mary's words had opened up a whole new area of hurt of which till then, I had been unaware. Of course I wasn't the only one concerned. I had been so turned in on myself and my own misery ever since that all-enveloping depression had hit me that I had completely ignored all the consequent ripples that were endlessly swirling out in every direction, especially in my own immediate family—reaching and touching and maybe even submerging people I loved.

My two sudden departures for that psychiatric clinic must have totally disrupted our home life and affected the children, shattering or certainly damaging their security. They couldn't possibly have understood what was happening at the time. And I wondered grimly how many more people were going to be hurt before I had finished.

As my thoughts cascaded round and round, eddying in an endless, incomprehensible tide, I remembered once again Jacques' words to me when I had agonized over the decision I had to make: the decision to put an end "for medical reasons"—my own mental health reasons—to the life of the baby I longed to have. And my heart went out in gratitude to the man I had married who had shown such love and understanding, and who had been prepared to accept the consequences of my going ahead and having the baby.

But then I hadn't counted on my husband's deep faith, which at the time I did not share. He had had that personal encounter with Jesus and placed his life and the lives of those he loved in his Savior's hands. And that made all the difference. He could say with equanimity that he was pre-pared to face the consequences knowing that whatever happened, Jesus would be by his side to guide and strengthen him. Remembering this, for a fraction of a sec-ond I faltered and almost changed my mind, deciding to throw in my lot with my husband's. But the moment passed and with it the opportunity to reverse a decision that was to haunt me for a long time to come. Only being a good churchgoer and not having had that spiritual encounter, I did not know how to cast this immense bur-den on Jesus. And, carrying it alone, I knew that it was more than I could bear.

"You're right," I said at last to Mary, rousing myself from my thoughts.

And I turned and hugged her.

"You may be 'only an old maid,'" I said quietly, "but you've got a wisdom and an insight that far outweighs many mothers' and grandmothers' I know. Far outweighs mine, in any case. Until you opened my eyes, it had never occurred to me how hurt my parents could be if they found out."

Mary looked up and her eyes were bright. They had in them the same expression I had noticed in Sister B.'s eyes the day before. I could see that my hug had touched her, that she wasn't used to shows of affection. And I wondered again why we British had been brought up "not to touch," only to present the stiff upper lip and not to show spontaneous love and warmth, why we felt it necessary to strangle the natural emotions in us that so often longed to be released.

"There," she said, to hide her embarrassment, "that's finished."

She folded the exquisite piece of needlework and put it in a work basket on the table at her elbow.

"Mary," I marveled, picking it up and holding it out, "it's beautiful. Do you do much of this kind of thing?"

"Haven't you noticed the seats on the dining room chairs?" she inquired, "and all the cushions in here?"

I had, but I hadn't realized that it was all her work.

"How clever," I murmured. "I'd love to be able to sew like that."

"Would you really?" she asked. "Then why don't you? It's not difficult."

"I wouldn't have the faintest idea how to start," I laughed.

"Then I'll show you," she said, getting up and smoothing her skirt. "Tomorrow's Thursday. You don't have to be back to the hospital till Friday, so why don't we do something? There's an exhibition at the National Gallery I've been meaning to go to. Would it interest you?"

"Lovely," I replied enthusiastically, welcoming something that might provide a distraction from my morbid thoughts.

"Well then, let's go in the morning, have lunch somewhere nice in town, and on the way back we can pop into Peter Jones and get you some tapestry to work on. Then we can come home, sit by the fire, and I'll show you how to do it."

I relaxed and leaned back against the sofa, feeling a vague semblance of peace. A day's outing with no worries and then a long, cozy evening sitting snugly by the fire in this lovely room and learning a craft was an enticing prospect.

Mary noticed my release of tension.

"Keeping your hands busy creating something beautiful will keep your mind from dwelling on things less beautiful," she remarked.

She stooped to put the guard in front of the fire.

"But first things first," she smiled, straightening up. "If we don't go down to dinner soon, it will be ruined. Give you five minutes to comb your hair."

I ran up the narrow flight of stairs into my little bedroom. Mary's words had plunged me back into the far-off days of my childhood. They reminded me of my grandmother, who had always been very strict about my combing my hair before coming to the table. And the feeling of being a carefree little girl again was delightful.

four

W hen I walked into the now familiar consulting room just before lunch on Friday morning, Professor Ponting was waiting with Simon Wing and a man I had never seen before.

The professor smiled and motioned me to a seat.

"You know Dr. Wing," he said, "and this is Dr. Benson."

We nodded in each other's direction as the professor looked down at the papers on his desk.

I felt as if I were at an inquisition and was momentarily angry at the doctors in Paris who had led me to believe that "abortion on demand" was the current thing in London—that all I had to do was walk through the doors of any hospital, push a button, and be aborted on the spot. I was glad they were wrong, but couldn't help wondering how many other women had been led astray by them. Perhaps women who, like myself, had been pressured into making a decision they were not sure was the right one. And who, following the doctor's advice, would subsequently find themselves alone in a foreign country, not only unfamiliar with the customs but possibly unfamiliar with the language as well. Women who would not have the feeling of security I had of being on home ground.

The professor's voice broke in on my ponderings.

"We have discussed your case very thoroughly," I heard him say, "and feel that in the circumstances, taking into account your past history, it would be better to terminate this pregnancy."

I bit my lip. Conflicting emotions were in my throat battling for a hearing. As they strove to reach the surface, I closed my lips tightly, afraid of the words that might come.

Professor Ponting looked up inquiringly over the rim of his glasses. Had he taken my silence as a sign that I had changed my mind?

"Of course," he said gently, "the decision is yours. We can only advise. If you wish for time to reconsider…"

"No," I answered tightly, "I don't think so."

He looked down at the papers on his desk. His two colleagues were both staring at the floor.

"In that case," he continued, "if you would like to come in on Monday, I will operate the next day."

By now time had ceased to have any meaning.

I had expected to be on my way home today, so the fact that he was proposing to operate in the middle of next week was neither here nor there. I had vaguely hoped that it might be Monday so that I could at least gain one day, but at the point where I stood now—Monday or Tuesday—what did it matter?

"Thank you," I replied, not knowing what else to say.

He shuffled the papers together. "I'm afraid I won't know until you are on the table whether I shall have to make an incision—do the operation abdominally or not. You've left it rather late, I'm afraid."

I knew that only too well and nodded numbly.

"I'll do my best not to. But you'll just have to trust me and give me leave to do whatever has to be done."

"Of course," I said, my eyes fixed on the floor.

We had now come down to cold, hard clinical facts. And it was horrible.

Before it had just been a word. Now the technicalities were spread out on the desk in front of me. Admission date, ward, blood group, medication. It was no longer a theory, something which had been advised by many qualified people, no longer an abstract word. Now I was down to practical details. And I shrank from the final reality.

The professor stood up and his two colleagues sprang to attention. He walked around the side of the desk and, to my surprise, took my arm as I, too, got up.

"If, on the other hand, you change your mind and decide to keep this baby," he said, leading me toward the door, "then we will do everything in our power to help you."

Was he giving me a loophole?

I looked up at him.

"How *can* you help me?" I whispered. "You are here in London and I live in France. There's twenty-two miles of water between us."

He nodded sympathetically. "I agree," he replied. "But there are good doctors in France as well, you know." And he smiled.

"They advised me to come over here," I answered curtly. And I turned toward the door, the conversation definitely terminated. There didn't seem to be any point in going round and round in any more circles.

"Thank you for your kindness, Professor," I said. "Good-bye, Dr. Benson. Good-bye, Dr. Wing."

Simon Wing looked at me roguishly and grinned. "Good-bye Nurse B." He smiled and we all laughed, breaking the tension that had threatened to cloud our closing conversation.

I went upstairs and back into the long corridor and dialed Mary's number.

"I'm just off to Essex," I announced, "but I'm coming back on Monday for the operation on Tuesday."

"I'll be thinking of you...and I know your parents will be delighted that you've come home."

"I hope so," I replied.

"I know so," laughed Mary. "Oh, by the way, Charlotte phoned just after you left. She apparently called her brother

Robert who said he and Dinah will be delighted to have you stay for a few days when you get out of the hospital so that you can get your strength back before returning home."

"How kind," I murmured.

"You're more than welcome to come back here," Mary went on, "but Charlotte thought that since they live in the country, it would be more of a convalescence than climbing up and down my stairs."

"Oh, Mary," I exclaimed, suddenly overwhelmed by all this love that was being showered on me. "You are a darling. Thank you so much for all you've done for me. Not only putting me up, but all the rest. I'll never be able to repay you."

"Nonsense," she replied firmly. "Just get on and finish that needlepoint. I'll be cross if you waste all the time I spent teaching you."

We both laughed.

"Good-bye, dear Mary," I said at last. "Thank you for both your invitations, but I think I'll just go straight home. It can't be easy for Jacques managing without me, and I rather hope the children are missing me. I want to get back to them as soon as possible. I've already been away far longer than expected."

"I understand," she answered.

"I knew you would," I breathed, and we both hung up. Those three days away from the normal, everyday cares of my own home and away from the nagging torment of trying to make a decision that I knew I could easily regret had calmed me and given me a new perspective.

I realized that I was almost able to laugh again.

The decision had at last been made, and as far as I could see, there was no going back. In a way, I was thankful. Thankful that the whole agonizing business would soon be behind me.

I looked up and found myself standing outside the hospital chapel. As I had done a few months earlier in a little old church in a French village, without knowing why, I walked in.

The chapel was cold and empty and smelled musty. But it hadn't changed. I sat down abruptly on a hard wooden pew at the back and remembered the times I had come here in years past, the patients I had wheeled in or helped to the services, the impressive array of nurses and sisters and doctors in white coats who had been there on Sunday mornings.

As I remembered, I felt the slender thread that held me to the past and those truths I had been brought up with. And as in that little French church, an immense peace once again flooded through me, and I felt that a hospital like this, one that was founded on and soaked in prayer, could not be one where its members made mistakes.

Comforted, I rose from my knees and crept out, closing the heavy door silently behind me.

five

The train crawled through the sordid outskirts of the east end of London, bleak high-rise buildings junketing for position with the remnants of former tenements where gray laundry still showed at some of the grimy windows.

It wasn't yet the rush hour and every little station beckoned us to a halt. Hordes of small boys just let out from school were swarming down the mean streets shrieking with the sheer joy of living. In the concrete courtyards of the depressing blocks of flats, games of football were in progress.

I had bought an evening paper, but it lay unread on my lap as I watched London snake past. As I gazed vacantly through the carriage window, a tousle-haired little boy sitting on a wall at the end of a slum easement area grinned at me and waved. I waved back, and as I did so, my mind went to Christopher. And I wondered what he had thought when he woke on Tuesday morning and found I had gone. He certainly wouldn't understand. And suddenly, as the outskirts of London gave way to the flat brown earth of

Essex, my fragile peace was threatened once again.

Getting off the train, I felt the sharp, fresh tang of a sea wind on my face. As I walked out of the station and up the hill toward the church, the old clock in the tower struck the hour. I passed through the lichen gate and cut across the churchyard, and as I did so, I saw a light shining from my parents' drawing room window, sending a pool of orange into the gathering dusk. I hastened my steps. It hadn't occurred to me to wonder whether they would be home or not. I just took it for granted that they were always there, and it crossed my mind that perhaps I had taken them for granted too.

As I turned in at the gate and slowly went up the path, I saw my father come to the window and draw the heavy curtains against the January night. Suddenly the warm interior was shut out, with only a small sliver of light showing through the chink. I ran up the steps and rang the bell and stood waiting as I heard the drawing room door open and my father's footsteps in the hall.

He opened the door, blinking in amazement when he saw me standing there. Then, just as Mary had done a few days before, he flung it wide in a gesture of welcome, standing aside to let me in.

"It's Noreen," he called joyously to my mother, who in turn came into the hall.

I was now out of the sharp sea wind and the cold, dark night and into the warmth and love of my family.

"We're just having tea," my mother said as I stopped to kiss her. "I'll fetch another cup."

My father took my coat and ushered me into the firelit room. It had the familiar smell of old roses and lavender, which grew in profusion under the window in summer and seemed to linger in the room all year round, and I knew without glancing at the tea tray that there would be homemade dundee cake. As I had done as a child, I flopped down on the pouf in front of the fire—also Bee's favorite seat whenever she was here.

My father looked over his shoulder at the door and came over to me. "I didn't say anything to your mother," he whispered, "but I knew you were here."

I looked up in amazement. How could he have possibly known?

"I happened to be at the bank on Tuesday afternoon when they telephoned through from a London branch where you'd gone to cash that check I sent you for Christmas."

I still looked puzzled.

"I suppose it was a slip on the cashier's part," continued my father, "but he'd just taken the call when I walked in and obviously thinking I knew you were over, he said, 'So you've got your daughter home again.'"

Now it was clear to me and I looked up at my father inquiringly.

"I didn't want to embarrass him," he went on, "so I

gave the impression that I knew. But I must say I've been rather worried. I realized you hadn't the children with you and I couldn't imagine what you were doing by yourself. Then when you didn't telephone…"

He stopped as my mother came back into the room, and I mentally sent up thanks to Mary for her insight in persuading me to come.

"I'll explain later," I hissed, and he nodded.

"What are you two whispering about?" My mother smiled.

"Just inquiring if your dundee cake is up to standard," I replied.

"Try it and see," she said, sitting down in her wing chair by the tea tray and lifting the teapot.

Nothing had changed; everything was as it had always been. Tea by the fire, the curtains drawn against the winter's night and the clock ticking peacefully on the mantelpiece. I was grateful for the security it represented. And I knew I could relax. At the time it didn't strike me as odd that my parents hadn't asked why I was there alone and unannounced. It was all so timeless and peaceful that I was content to just sit back and enjoy it and leave the explanations until later.

"How are the children?" my mother asked as she poured me a second cup of tea. It seemed that hours had passed since I flopped down in front of the fire and soaked up the peace and familiarity of it all. Now I was ready to

talk, to tell them why I was here…and to face the consequences. The story came tumbling out and they listened
without interrupting me and without comment.

"I never did fully understand why you were in that
clinic last summer," my mother said when I had finished.
"And then when you had to go back again…"

My parents only knew that Christopher was a beautiful nine-pound baby and that we were thrilled by his
arrival.

They didn't know about the resultant depression and
breakdown that had forced me into the psychiatric clinic
six months after his birth; Jacques had not felt it necessary
to cause them pain and worry then, and I didn't feel it was
the time to inflict the details on them now.

"It was all very upsetting," she said at last.

"I'm sorry," I answered lamely. "I'm sure it must have
been, but I suppose Jacques wanted to spare you the
worry."

She sighed. "Sometimes children cause more worry by
trying to spare their parents than if they told them the
truth," she replied.

My mother was by no means a career woman or a
woman of the world. She had lived a sheltered life, giving all
her time and considerable artistic talent to her home and
family. Yet like Mary, she was strangely wise and could come
out with some surprisingly profound statements at times.

There was an awkward silence. My father gazed into

the fire, saying nothing. He seemed crushed by the news.

"Did your brother know?" my mother inquired a minute or so later, and I knew from her voice that her former statement had only been prompted by love and concern and not by irritation or resentment as I had at first thought.

"Yes," I answered. "You were staying with them when Olivier brought Yves over to Germany after I was taken into the clinic for the first time."

"I remember," she replied, "but he and Sylvie rather played it down when we wanted to know more." She sighed again.

"I suppose you all did it for the best," she concluded. "This conspiracy of silence. You and Geoffrey were always as thick as thieves, even as children."

"I suppose we still are," I said, smiling.

"I'm glad," she murmured. "It's nice to know it's lasted."

She smiled to herself as we lapsed into a comfortable silence. I knew she was thinking of her own younger brother with whom she had always had a very strong link like the one that existed between Geoffrey and me. And perhaps remembering, she understood.

My father stirred in his chair and looked up at last. "When do you go back to the hospital?" he asked.

"On Monday," I replied. "The operation will be on Tuesday."

"And afterwards?" he went on. "Can you come back here and recuperate?"

"I'd rather get back home," I answered. "I'm worried about the children so I wouldn't rest. And after all, it's not a major operation; I won't really need to convalesce."

He looked at me intently and made no comment, and once again, I was suddenly overwhelmed by the immense kindness being shown by all those around me, by the unconditional love and nonjudgmental attitudes. I had half expected the world to come down on me like a ton of bricks, accusing and condemning. Maybe I would have found it easier if they had; I could have fought back. But everywhere I went I had met with both sympathy and understanding.

My parents hadn't said anything. Perhaps their English reserve kept them from showing their feelings. I don't know. They never did say anything; they spared me and kept their hurt to themselves. Yet to them it must have been a shock and a blow. But if it was, my bombshell in no way altered our relationship. They just continued to love me as they had always done.

I realized once again the enormity of the ripples that I had caused by tossing that one pebble into the still, untroubled water. Ripples that I could not control, but for which I was responsible. I understood the truth of the saying "No man is an island." Whatever we do has consequences that rebound, sometimes not only in our own lifetime but from one generation to the next.

The clock in the hall wheezed and prepared to strike the hour, breaking the silence of that well-loved room.

"I think I'll go upstairs and change," I said, getting up.

My mother picked up her knitting from the little embroidered bag hanging on the arm of her chair.

"I expect you're tired," she said.

"A little," I replied, "but I'll have an early night, and then I'll feel on top of the world in the morning."

I turned in the doorway, wanting to show them my gratitude but not knowing how.

"Thank you for not judging me," I murmured lamely.

My mother looked up from her knitting and looked away again. My father continued to gaze into the fire, his paper lying unread on his lap. I felt again that barrier of reserve that I had not noticed when I had lived this side of the Channel—that fear of expressing emotion, of showing one's feelings. I was sorry I couldn't say more. But I knew they understood what I meant, and I was grateful for their unconditional acceptance of me.

six

I awoke next morning to see a thin streak of frosty sunshine creeping through the chink in the curtains and falling onto the foot of my bed. The wind of the previous evening had dropped, driving before it the rain that had dampened my stay in London, and Saturday dawned bright and cold. I turned lazily to look at my clock and saw a cup of tea cooling on the bedside table. Nine fifteen. I had almost slept around the clock!

My father appeared in the doorway with a fresh cup of tea and came and sat on the bed.

"We thought we'd let you sleep," he said. "Your breakfast is on its way up."

"Oh no," I protested. "I'm getting up."

"But why?" he smiled. "Take things easy while you can. Have your breakfast leisurely and get up when you're ready."

He crossed the room to draw back the curtains, letting the silver strand of winter sunshine trickle into the room.

"It's a lovely day," he announced, looking out on the

garden, and I smiled to myself at his British optimism. It was bitterly cold, freezing, in fact. I could see the icicles outside the window pane and the glint of frost on the roof of the garden shed, but to him it was a "lovely day."

"We were wondering whether you would like to do something?"

He turned back into the room as I sat up and sipped my tea.

"What were you thinking of?" I asked.

"Well," he replied, "it's not often you are here on your own and we thought perhaps you'd like to go out for the day. We could drive into the country and have lunch somewhere, then make our way back in time for tea."

"Lovely idea," I answered.

"Right," he said. "Your breakfast will be here in a minute. Get up when you want and we'll leave when you're ready. No hurry, we've got all day."

I lay back on my pillows and yawned, reveling in the luxury of having a day with no appointments, no grueling decisions to make, nothing to do but relax and enjoy it.

The evening before I had spoken to Jacques on the telephone and told him of the latest developments and had his assurance that everything was running smoothly at home. The younger ones had taken it in stride, as children so often do, the fact that I was no longer around, and Yves and Bee reminded him hourly of his promise of popcorn and a trip on the lake, and they were planning the outing for

Saturday afternoon. "Relax and enjoy yourself," were his parting words.

This bright winter morning I sat up in bed and decided to do just that.

On Sunday morning, we crossed the garden to the solemn clang of the last bell and walked over to the Norman church I knew so well. It was a beautiful church, and that morning the vicar took for his text a passage from Isaiah 26.

"Thou wilt keep him in perfect peace, whose mind is stayed on Thee: because he trusteth in Thee. Trust ye in the Lord for ever: for in the Lord Jehovah is everlasting strength."

I don't remember much about the sermon, but those verses he quoted kept circling round and round in my brain, and I had the feeling they were meant just for me. I so needed peace from the crushing problems that had been dragging me down into a black pit for months. I needed strength to face the days ahead, but above all, I needed someone Almighty in whom I could trust. What I really needed was to sit back and take stock of my life, to face it squarely instead of exhausting myself running away from something I couldn't easily define. But I knew I couldn't do it by myself: I needed to have my mind stayed on him. But where was he?

I only knew him as a tragic figure in a stained-glass window or through the pages of the ivory-backed prayer book I had been given at my confirmation all those years ago. No one had ever presented Jesus to me as a living person.

As the vicar stood in the porch after the service, greeting his parishioners, I asked him for the reference for his text. And so unfamiliar was I with the Bible at that time that I remember wondering, as we walked out into the old graveyard, where to look for the book of Isaiah, puzzling as to whether it was in the Old Testament or New!

I didn't realize then, but those two verses quoted from the pulpit that bright January Sunday morning were to follow and encourage me in the difficult months ahead. Nothing happens by chance in our lives; I am convinced of that now. Since I became a committed Christian, what people call "coincidences" I like to think of as "God-incidences." I am sure that God put those words into the vicar's mouth so that, in spite of the fact that I was grieving him by what I intended to do, his love was unconditional. I would be given peace and be drawn by that invisible thread that had always held me to Jesus, although I didn't know it at the time. A thread that was to draw me ever closer, until a few months later I would burst from the dark cocoon in which I had been living and acknowledge him as my Lord and Savior.

That afternoon as my mother and I sat in a companionable silence in front of the drawing room fire, she with her knitting and me with my newly acquired tapestry, the sun, high in the sky, splashing through the low west-facing windows and sending pale sunbeams dancing on the deep blue carpet, those words came back to me again: "Thou wilt keep him in perfect peace, whose mind is stayed on Thee: because he trusteth in Thee. Trust ye in the Lord for ever: for in the Lord Jehovah is everlasting strength."

There in that familiar room I indeed felt at peace, and I longed to "trust in the Lord," but I didn't know how to go about it.

My mother had taken Geoffrey and me to church from our earliest childhood, but the litany had been merely a ritual, something I stood up and chanted with the rest of the congregation. The childhood prayers I had learned and repeated dutifully at my bedside each evening, the beautiful words of the *Common Prayer Book,* which I knew by heart and which now reveal such depths of worship for me just didn't, at that moment, measure up to what I needed.

I sought restlessly for a way to meet my Lord, but the way seemed barred. He was still only that beautiful tragic figure in a stained-glass window, and all I could do was repeat silently, "Thou wilt keep him in perfect peace whose mind is stayed on Thee; because he trusteth in Thee,"— and gain comfort from the fact that wherever he was, he knew I longed to trust in him—and hope that one day he would reveal himself to me.

The weekend passed too quickly and the dreaded Monday was upon me almost before I realized it. But I met it with less fear than I had expected.

The glorious promise of spring hinted at during the weekend didn't last, and Monday morning found us sitting at the breakfast table with a sharp wind whipping through the trees in the garden and the low, gray skies threatening rain to come.

"I won't drive you to London," my father began as my mother got up to answer the telephone.

I started to protest that it wasn't necessary.

"What I'm trying to say," he went on patiently, "is that it would be hopeless by car and far quicker by rail. So I've decided to come with you on the train and see you safely installed."

I saw through his words to the concern behind them and I didn't want to hurt him by refusing his offer. But I felt able to cope with what lay ahead and didn't want him to waste his day on a journey that was not in the least bit necessary.

"Please don't," I said quietly. "I'd really much rather go on my own. After this lovely weekend, I feel so much better than when I arrived. And what's the point? To come all that way just to leave me at the hospital gate."

He looked at me sharply. "I think your mother would feel happier if I did," he answered hesitantly.

She was still on the telephone and hadn't heard our discussion, and I was anxious to settle the question before she joined us.

"Mothers always fuss," I laughed, getting up from the table. "I know I do. But honestly, it isn't necessary. And anyway, I must be off in half an hour."

My father saw I was adamant and wisely didn't insist.

"I'll walk down to the station with you," he said at last. "Your bag's not very heavy so there's no point in taking the car, and the fresh air will do us both good."

I smiled at him, grateful once more for his understanding.

When I walked through the gate of the hospital I knew exactly where to go. It was a small unit apart from the main building, and I had worked there during my second year in training.

I wondered whether Sidney the old porter would still be in his little cubbyhole. He wasn't. There was a much younger man sitting there who treated me kindly but with the same kindness he would have shown to any other patient—not the effusive greeting I would have received from Sidney.

"There you are at last!"

A familiar voice broke in on my dreaming as I sat waiting to be taken to my ward. I looked up, then leapt to my feet with joy.

"Judy!"

The sister-in-charge laughed and stooped to pick up my bags.

"Simon Wing told me you were to be admitted, and

I've been on the lookout for you for the last two hours."

She took my arm and led me along the corridor and up the stairs, dropping my case to open the door to her small office-cum-sitting room.

"I've asked for lunch to be served here, just the two of us," she said, motioning me to an armchair by the electric fire. "Once you're in the ward we won't have much time together, and I thought it would be nice to have a chat and catch up on news first."

She placed a small table between us as lunch was brought in on a tray.

I looked around the small room with the high, narrow windows, identical to the one every sister had attached to her ward, yet each one made different by the marks of her own personality. My eyes fell on the well-worn Bible lying on her desk, and I saw the plain wooden cross hanging on the wall above it. Judy hadn't changed. She must still have that deep, unshakable faith that I remembered.

She and I had arrived at the hospital training school on the same day, a bright windy Saturday toward the end of March, and had lived and worked together for four years. At one point, when we were working in the country at one of the hospital's outposts, we had even shared a room. I particularly remembered with gratitude her gentleness, her serenity, and her shining faith.

I glanced at Judy, sitting placidly opposite me, and marveled that she looked exactly the same as on that first day. There was hardly a wrinkle on her smooth, powder-free face, the only difference was the tall sister's cap with the bow under the chin sitting sedately on her unruly chestnut curls. Then I noticed a streak of gray running through the black strands.

"Tell me what's been happening with you," I said as she poured the coffee.

"Tell me what has been happening with *you,*" she laughed. "You're the one who's been doing things. I haven't moved."

"You've only to read my notes to find out what's been happening to me," I answered dryly.

She looked up and her hazel eyes were full of compassion.

"I *have* read them," she said quietly. "I'm so sorry, Bertie."

Bertie had been my hospital nickname. No one had called me that for years. And suddenly, I felt like crying. But if they had spilled over, I think they would have been tears of relief, sheer relief that, with Judy—as with Mary—I didn't have to pretend that all was well. That life was beautiful. That I hadn't a care in the world as I had been attempting to do with my friends ever since Christopher's birth. Trying to cover up the rot and even convince myself that the black thoughts I was thinking weren't real. I could drop the mask and be myself. Judy knew me. She had read my notes. She knew why I was here, and like Mary and my parents, she didn't condemn me.

Why was I so afraid of what people would think? Why was I so convinced that everyone would come down with a sledgehammer and attack me?

There was a knock at the door and a student nurse came quietly in.

"We're ready to report, Sister," she said respectfully, hands behind her back, eyes downcast, just as I had done so many times in the past before going off duty.

I smiled at Judy and she smiled back, reading my thoughts.

"Just like old times, isn't it?" I volunteered as the nurse withdrew.

"In a way," Judy reminisced. "But a lot of things have changed. They have much more freedom than we had."

"Couldn't have been less," I remarked, and we both laughed, remembering.

"They still squirm under the yoke, though, like we used to do."

"*You* never did," I retorted. "You were always the perfect nurse. I was the one who kicked and squirmed."

"Perhaps, but you were a lot of fun, Bertie," she ended. "I don't know how our set would have survived without you."

I was pleased by the compliment. It cheered me up and made me think. I'd admired Judy because she was so quiet and efficient and she'd admired me because I was most of the time pretty inefficient but "a lot of fun."

"The sisters didn't always think so," I laughed.

Judy got up and we went out into the corridor, the antiseptic smell striking with greater force after the delicate scent of potted hyacinths that lingered in Judy's little room.

She showed me into a ward with six beds in it, five of which were already occupied. The sixth was in an alcove made by the window and Judy put my case down beside it.

"You'd better get undressed and lie down," she said apologetically. "They'll be coming round to do some tests soon."

The idea of going to bed at two o'clock in the afternoon was sheer bliss: she needn't have felt apologetic at all. Anyway, I had been bitten by the tapestry bug and couldn't wait to get out my needle again.

"Don't need to show you the ropes," Judy said. "You know where everything is. Just relax and make yourself comfortable, and I'll see you later."

She made no attempt to introduce me to the other occupants of the room, for which I was grateful. If we wanted to talk and get acquainted, we could do so by ourselves, but if we just felt like keeping quiet, that was all right too. Two of the women were dozing, one was flicking through a magazine, another was knitting furiously as if her whole life depended on it, and the fifth was standing in her dressing gown, gazing out the window. I supposed that, like me, they were all new admissions and didn't feel inclined to chatter at the moment.

I didn't see Judy the rest of the afternoon, though I was aware of her presence in and out of the four small wards under her charge. Once or twice I heard her quiet voice through the open doorway of our ward. After supper was cleared away, a trickle of visitors started to come through the door and pull up chairs beside each bedside. I busied myself with my tapestry, quite content to be alone and listen to the soft buzz of conversation all around me and the faint rustle of paper bags as husbands and mothers discharged fruit and other goodies into the bedside lockers.

It was after the visitors were gone and the nurses had come in to shake up the pillows and tidy the beds for the night and silence had once more descended on the ward that Judy came in and went from bed to bed exchanging a few words with each patient. When she came to me, she pulled up a chair and sat down.

"How are you feeling?" she asked.

"I'm perfectly all right," I answered truthfully. For indeed I was.

The peace of the weekend still lingered, and the agonizing of the previous weeks had almost disappeared.

"Do you often have cases like mine?" I asked her.

"Hardly ever," Judy replied. "Professor Ponting is a fine man, and he doesn't agree to do this operation lightly. He only ever operates in exceptional cases. After all, the abortion law hasn't been passed yet, and he takes a great risk doing it at all."

She paused and looked straight at me.

"The fact that he advised termination means that it should be done," she ended quietly.

I was silent for a moment.

"What do you think?" I asked at last.

Judy hesitated. "I'm not a mother," she replied at last, "but…yes, I believe you're doing the right thing."

She got up and patted my hand. "Do you think you'll be able to sleep?"

"Like a log." I smiled.

"If you can't, don't hesitate to call the nurse on duty. Even if it's too late for a sedative she can always make you a cup of cocoa."

She looked at me in surprise when I burst out laughing, not immediately realizing the significance of her statement.

"That's the phrase that reminded Simon Wing and me where we'd met before."

Judy smiled.

"Three A.M. cocoa and bread and marg in the ward kitchen," she said, laughing. "How well I remember."

"I'll just have the cocoa," I teased. "Don't bother about the bread and marg."

"*Butter* now," she laughed again. "And sugar in the cocoa. Rationing is over."

And with that lighthearted remark, she walked noise-lessly out of the ward.

seven

⁓

True to my word I did "sleep like a log" and was only awakened when the early morning tea trolley came round at six-thirty. I had surprised even myself and lay there thinking of nothing in particular as I considered getting up and having a bath before my "light breakfast" would be brought to me.

At about ten o'clock Professor Ponting walked into the ward and came and sat down by my bed. He picked up the piece of tapestry and admired it.

"Very pretty," he remarked, putting it down. "And how do you feel this morning?"

"Rested," I said laconically, returning his smile.

"No regrets?"

"No regrets."

"Very well then, we shall meet again later on."

He got up and stood looking down at me.

"But if ever you do have second thoughts between now and then, you are perfectly at liberty to get up and leave the hospital. No one will say anything, and no one will think any the worse of you."

I bit my lip. Was he once again offering me a way out? I wondered. And for a split second I wavered, as all my suppressed maternal feelings that I had been unsuccessfully trying to push into the background rose up and cried out to me to get up and go. But I didn't have the strength that comes from perfect trust. And those verses that had echoed in that little Norman church only two days before were still only words and not a reality in my life.

"Thank you," I whispered unsteadily, "but I think we'll meet upstairs all the same."

I picked up my tapestry and bent my head to hide those wretched tears that were threatening yet again to come cascading down my cheeks.

The morning passed swiftly and just as the sound of the lunch trolley was heard in the corridor, Judy came with a young nurse to give me my injection.

"I'll be coming with you when you go upstairs," she said comfortingly. "Just lie back now and try to sleep."

I nodded gratefully. It was kind of her to come with me, but it was no more than I would have expected of Judy. And with those thoughts in my mind, I seemed to float off somewhere above the bed. My body felt light and transparent and any anguish or fear or apprehension I might formerly have experienced evaporated.

I was vaguely aware of the porters lifting me onto the

gurney and of Judy's stiff white cuff close to my chin gently guiding the gurney along the corridor and into the elevator. As we entered the small anesthetic room, a pale sun came streaming in through the uncurtained window.

"Lovely day," I murmured drowsily.

"It is a lovely day," Judy replied from somewhere far away. "Quite a change from yesterday."

The door quietly opened, and I was aware of a green-gowned figure standing above me.

"Hallo, Bertie," he said.

I blinked open my eyes and looked up into a face that was vaguely familiar.

"It's Adrian," Judy explained. "He's your anesthetist."

He smiled and once again the memories came flooding back.

"Adrian," I murmured drowsily, "of course."

Another face from the past. Another link with Simon Wing and Judy and the old days. How good God was to bring all these comforting little strands back into my life at this time. How good… I felt my arm being held by a strong hand and a prick as the needle slipped into my vein, and I drifted away on another cloud, completely unaware at the time that in my semiconscious state I had attributed all these "coincidences" to God, that I had acknowledged his goodness and the fact that he cared for me down to each little detail in my life.

Had I known my Bible then as I know it now, Romans

8:28 would surely have blazoned itself on my mind: "And we know that in all things God works for the good of those who love Him."

Out of this evil to which I had consented, the murder of my unborn child, which was certainly not part of his perfect plan for my life, God was trying to bring good by leading me onward, nearer to him, nearer to that new life he promises to all who believe in him.

Was my baby's death to be the catalyst that opened my eyes to the truth, to Jesus?

If so, it was a terrible price to pay.

———

Piles of soft clouds billowed round me as I strove sleepily to rise above them. I heard the murmur of voices in the ward and, half opening my eyes, noticed that there was still a little sunshine coming through the top of the tall windows and splashing on the walls. A warm wave washed over me and I floated back into its gentle sway. I felt a light touch on my arm and, forcing open my eyes, once more saw Judy standing beside me, her cool fingers on my wrist, a large old-fashioned pocket watch in her other hand.

"Is it over?" I murmured sleepily.

"Yes, all over," she answered quietly.

"Did you stay with me?"

"Until you went into the operating room," she replied, "then I was waiting to bring you down afterward."

"Thank you."

She released my wrist as another wave of sleep washed over me and I closed my eyes.

"Was it a boy or a girl?" I slurred, the words coming out thickly through the enveloping haze of the anesthetic.

Judy bent to smooth the sheet under my chin.

"It's best not to know," she said softly, and as I sank back down into the depths of blissful unconsciousness, she tiptoed away.

When I opened my eyes again, there was no longer any sunlight in the ward. The lights were on and the clatter of dishes told me that the supper things were being cleared away.

With a sudden gesture of fear, my hand went to my abdomen. But there was no swathe of bandages, only the feel of warm skin untouched by a knife under the cotton operation gown. I struggled to sit up and blinked around me. Once again Judy appeared as if from nowhere, this time with a bowl of water, which she placed on the locker by my bed before fetching a screen.

"Feeling better?" she asked.

I nodded.

"Feeling more alive," I replied. "You kept fading away last time I saw you."

"You hadn't been down long," Judy explained. "Your husband has just phoned and your father and a Miss Myers called about half an hour ago. They all send you their love."

Once again I had that warm feeling inside me. So much kindness. I had expected my family to inquire, but Mary…well, perhaps it was what I would have expected from Mary, too. Dear Mary, I thought as I tried to struggle to a sitting position.

Judy bent and gently drew me upward, slipping extra pillows behind my head.

"Now then," she said briskly, "let's get rid of that gown and put you in your own nightie again. You'll feel much better after I've freshened you up."

Obediently I allowed myself to be washed and dressed, then sank thankfully back on to the mound of pillows Judy had so expertly arranged for me.

"Funny to be this side of the blanket," I remarked.

"Does us all good at times," Judy replied.

I could hear the visitors beginning to wander in.

"I'll leave the screen round you for the time being," Judy murmured, clearing up the washing things.

I knew that her sensitive nature feared I would be upset to be on my own, the only patient without visitors.

But she needn't have worried.

"Now which would you prefer, a cup of clear soup or a cup of tea?" she asked.

"Tea, please," I replied.

"Better have it with lemon, not milk," she cautioned.

"That's all right," I answered. "I like it that way."

And she bustled off.

I lay there thinking of nothing in particular until Judy reappeared with a cup and saucer.

"There," she announced. "Drink that up, you can have a dry biscuit as well if you like."

I shook my head, sipping the tea gratefully, then looked at her over the rim of the thick hospital cup.

"Don't you *ever* go off duty?" I asked.

She smiled. "Sometimes," she answered, then added professionally, "I don't think you'd better have another cup; it might stop you from sleeping."

I grinned at her, but she didn't immediately see the joke.

"There's always hot cocoa," I teased.

The next day passed in a pleasant haze, and when on Thursday morning Professor Ponting came in followed by a cloud of students, I was beginning to feel restless.

He came over to me, leaving Dr. Benson and the students with a young woman who had been admitted the previous afternoon. As he sat down on my bed, I could hear the soft rise and fall of question and answer coming from behind the green-curtained screen.

"Well, and how are you feeling today?" he inquired pleasantly.

"I'm fine now," I replied, "and I'd like to go home."

He raised his eyebrows in surprise.

"So soon?" he asked.

"I've been away over a week…and I want to get back to the family."

"I understand that," he answered, fixing me with his piercing gray eyes. "But do you think you're fit enough?"

"I'm really feeling very well," I pleaded.

He stood up and looked through the window over the rooftops of London.

"You're feeling that way because you're in the hospital," he said at last. "But when you get home?"

He turned and his eyes pierced through me.

"I'm sure I'll be all right," I said, almost afraid to meet his gaze.

"I wish I could be as sure," he answered quietly. "Why not think about it, stay here and rest for a few days and go back home on Monday?"

"I want to go home tomorrow," I answered, feeling like a spoiled child pouting to get its own way.

For a moment he didn't say anything but stood stroking his chin. "It's a long journey," he announced at last. "Would you go back to Essex for the weekend if I agreed to your leaving tomorrow?"

"I want to go *home,*" I whispered, almost in tears.

He stood looking down at me from a great height.

"If you are *that* determined," he said, "I won't try to stop you. But it would be better not to rush things."

I didn't answer. I was afraid of my voice giving me away. The professor turned and walked over to the murmur of voices behind the screen.

I sat gazing down at the white bedspread with the cross

imprinted on the fabric, fighting back my tears and feeling threatened again by the overwhelming fear and despair that had accompanied me for so many months now and was hanging over me like a sword just waiting to drop. I fished under the pillow for a hankie and surreptitiously wiped the corners of my eyes, then picking up the tapestry, attacked the canvas viciously.

The professor and his team had left the ward, and I half hoped Judy would come in for a chat, but I didn't see her again until the middle of the afternoon when she came over and pulled up a chair by my bedside.

"Are you still determined to go home tomorrow?" she asked gently.

"Yes," I said tightly. And felt like a worm.

Everyone had been so kind to me, and here I was repaying them with a stubborn childish obstinacy, insisting on having my own way.

"I don't think it's very wise," she went on.

"*Judy,*" I pleaded, "I've got to go home. I left in a rush. I couldn't explain to the children. And apart from the odd phone call, I've no idea what's happening, how they are coping, or even worse, how they reacted to my rushing off like that."

"Your husband said on the telephone that everything was fine," she soothed.

I looked up and smiled tightly. "You don't know Jacques," I said grimly. "He ought to have gone into the diplomatic service. He's the most tactful man alive, and even if the house had been burnt to the ground and they were all living in a tent in the yard, he'd still have said everything was fine, so as not to worry me."

Judy said nothing and an awkward silence fell between us.

"*Please* Judy," I pleaded, "try to understand. I don't feel 100 percent, it's true, but I feel well enough to face the journey. And I'll not feel 100 percent until I get back home and start to pick up the threads of my life again."

"I *do* understand," she sighed. "Professor Ponting said he didn't think I'd be able to budge you, but I thought I'd have a try all the same."

She smiled as she got up. "I see I was right."

I smiled back. "Thanks, Judy," I said gratefully.

"I'll get everything ready for you to leave in the morning then. But promise me you'll see your doctor as soon as you get back and have him prescribe medication again. You feel all right now, but once you are home in the swing of things, it may be another matter...and we can't help then."

"More's the pity," I said. "You've been wonderful and helped me so much.... I'm sorry to behave like a spoiled brat."

Judy patted my hand. "You haven't," she said softly, "and I'm sure you'll be all right. Now what time does your train go? I'll get George to order a taxi."

"I think it's ten," I answered. "I'm not sure, but it's the Golden Arrow...."

"I'll find out," she answered with her usual efficiency. "Now just relax and rest.... You may not get the chance once you're back home."

I didn't see much of Judy before I left. The day had been particularly hectic for her with four of the five people admitted the previous day going up to the operating room. Apart from hearing her calm voice giving orders and soothing anxious patients, I sat on the fringe of things and watched. I went back down over the years again and remembered the frantic activity of a surgical ward on operating day. The suppressed haste with which we went about the mountain of jobs we were given to do, hysterically anxious on the inside because we were running late and cool, calm, and collected on the outside because the patients must never dream that we were in a frantic hurry or guess our inner turmoil.

Yes, I thought, it had been a good training, and my mind went back to Sister B., unflappable, imperturbable no matter what happened, and woe betide any one of us who happened to let slip the mask and show the least sign of stress or haste or even emotion. And as I watched the young nurses walking purposefully about, quietly, calmly, without haste, I smiled to myself, knowing what was going on on the inside.

Just before the lights were dimmed, Judy once more

came over to my bedside. She looked tired. It had been a very busy day, but in spite of it all, she was as much in control of the situation as ever, her apron crisp and rustling and her stiff white cuffs immaculate.

"Everything's ready for you to go tomorrow," she said quietly. "George is going to ring for a taxi at nine-thirty. The train leaves at ten so you should have plenty of time; we're only just round the corner from the station. You've got your ticket?"

I nodded.

"Then everything's settled," she said.

"You look tired," I said.

"It's been a busy day," she answered, stifling a yawn. "I won't be sorry to go to bed. Now you settle down and have a good night. You've got a long journey in front of you."

I snuggled back onto the pillows feeling relaxed and sleepy.

"Sleep well," Judy whispered as she turned out the light above my bed.

"You too," I whispered back, and silence fell on the ward.

eight

I was awake even before the early morning tea trolley began trundling round the ward. Knowing that I'd find Jacques still at home at that hour, I got up and went downstairs to telephone and let him know that I'd be arriving that afternoon.

It was as I put back the receiver that I saw a familiar figure in clerical black walking down the corridor toward me. We stared at each other, unbelieving. Then his lean face broke into a smile.

"What are *you* doing here?" he asked in surprise.

I smiled back. "Don't need to ask you that question," I replied, my eyes falling on the little black case he held in his hand. How many times had I seen him carry it into the wards during my years of training.

"I was called out during the night," he explained.

He looked inquiringly at me, and a wave of embarrassment swept over me as I suddenly became conscious of the fact that I was standing there in my dressing gown. I bit my lip and looked away.

"I've had a minor operation," I muttered, in answer to his unspoken question. "I'm going home this morning."

"To Paris?"

"Yes."

For a moment we stood there awkwardly, neither of us quite knowing what to say. Then he took my arm and drew me into the deserted waiting room.

As we sat down side by side on the hard bench, something in me wanted to get up and run away. Yet another part of me longed to tell him about the turmoil that had once again begun to boil up inside me the minute I saw his tall figure coming along the corridor.

Stephen and I had met when I was working with Judy at the only one of the hospital's wartime outposts that had somehow managed to survive the postwar era. He had been the local Catholic curate who was always in and out of the makeshift wards, comforting, cheering, encouraging, ministering to the patients. In fact, his understanding and compassion were so talked about around that small hospital that non-Catholic patients frequently asked to see him when they had a problem or were distressed or afraid of what the future might hold.

It was books that had brought us together. We were both voracious readers, and the hospital library being pretty limited, Stephen had offered me the run of his own considerable collection. Often when I was browsing through the shelves he would come in and we would sit and chat over a cup of tea. He never tried to convert me to Catholicism. But we often discussed spiritual matters and the various theories and doctrines that divided, and united, our two churches. Although I hadn't seen him since I went to Paris, we had kept in touch through Christmas cards.

Now, as I looked up, I saw that the young curate I had known had gone, and the busy, overworked parish priest he had become showed in the furrows on his forehead and the deep lines around his mouth.

Catching my eye, he smiled. And suddenly his whole expression changed and became boyish again. It was at that moment, almost without realizing what was happening, that I heard myself blurting out the reason for my being in the hospital.

"I've had a medical abortion," I stammered. "The specialists in Paris said it wasn't possible for me to have another baby…I'd lose my reason…be locked up in a mental home for the rest of my life, so I came here and…and the doctors agreed with them."

The words came tumbling out, falling crazily over one another as I sought to justify myself. I hoped he would say something to show that he understood, that he agreed. But he remained silent.

"It wasn't easy," I faltered at last.

"I'm sure it wasn't."

Stephen sat looking at the floor, neither condoning nor condemning.

"Do you think I was right?" I whispered. And even as I said it I knew what his answer would be.

"Do you?" I urged.

Stephen looked up and passed his hand over his eyes. But he avoided my gaze.

"I'm sure you thought you were doing the right thing," he said slowly. "And I'm sure the doctors who advised you have a high code of ethics."

He paused and seemed to be looking at something far in the distance, something I couldn't see.

"But what is the 'right thing?' The words seem to have a different meaning for different people."

He turned to look at me.

"Because it's possible to do a thing doesn't necessarily mean it's right," he said quietly. "It's very often something we ought *not* to do."

I knew now why I had had the urge to flee that sudden confusion of conflicting emotions inside me when I first saw him. I had known instinctively that he would not condone, could not condone what I had done; I put my hands up to cover my face.

"Why didn't I bump into you last Friday?" I said bitterly, "before it was too late?"

He didn't answer but sat staring at the floor.

"My own vicar said I had no choice," I went on grimly. "Just like the doctors did."

Stephen raised his blue-gray eyes and looked at me.

They were full of compassion, but I could read the message in them. The message that was to torture me for many months to come. It was as if he said, "But you *did* have a choice."

"The Bible says quite plainly," he went on gently, "that God knows us even before we are conceived, before we've taken any human shape at all."

I stared at him in amazement. "I didn't know that," I whispered.

"It's in Psalms," he replied, and taking a well-worn volume from his pocket, he turned the pages and quietly began to read:

> You created every part of me;
> You put me together in my mother's womb.
> I praise you because you are to be feared;
> all you do is strange and wonderful.
> I know it with all my heart.
> When my bones were being formed,
> carefully put together in my mother's womb,
> when I was growing there in secret,
> you knew that I was there—
> you saw me before I was born.
> The days allotted to me,
> had all been recorded in your book,
> before any of them ever began.
> (Psalm 139:13–16, TEV)

Those words shattered me. I felt the familiar lump rise in my throat and swallowed hard as my eyes misted over.

My baby was known to God, had been known to him for more than three months! Not only that, but God had prepared his or her future and planned each day…and I had destroyed that plan.

Stephen closed the book and slipped it back into his pocket.

"I wish I could say something to help you," he said sincerely. "But the Catholic Church feels very strongly on the whole issue. We believe a mother does not have the right to sacrifice her unborn child, even at the cost of her own life."

He looked at me with profound sadness and sympathy. "That can be a terrible decision to have to make," he ended quietly.

His face was strained and I realized that this was not a platitude or a doctrine he was repeating: it was obviously something about which he, too, felt very strongly. His words had cut deeply, but I felt that it had also hurt him to have to say what he did.

Into the painful silence, broken only by the slow, monotonous tick of the clock on the opposite wall, crashed the chimes of Big Ben striking the half hour.

Stephen rose wearily to his feet: he suddenly looked unbelievably tired.

"I have to go," he said. "I'm saying mass at eight-thirty."

He stooped to pick up his case and we stood looking at each other.

"*I'm* sorry we didn't meet last Friday too," he said softly.

I bit my lip.

"And I'm sorry you had to go through all this. I wish I could have helped you more."

"You *have* helped me," I answered quietly. "In the end, you may even have made things clear in my mind. So many people were trying to whitewash the situation."

Stephen passed his hand distractedly through his dark hair.

"If only you weren't leaving today, we could have talked somewhere quietly, in a more relaxed manner. Away from here."

He glanced around the bare, empty waiting room.

I nodded, but wondered whether it would have made any difference.

"It couldn't have changed anything," I answered brokenly.

"No," he said softly, "*we* couldn't. But our Lord can change everything."

He looked down at me with such care and concern in his eyes, and I knew he sensed my inner turmoil.

"Only *he* can bring you peace," he ended quietly. Squeezing my hand, he walked swiftly from the room.

When I got back to the ward, breakfast was in full swing—and so were my emotions.

As I pushed scrambled egg round the plate, my jumbled thoughts tossed in my mind like pieces of a jigsaw puzzle caught up in a tumble dryer, whirling helplessly round and round, trying to find their balance and fall into a pattern once again.

And I wondered bleakly if they ever would.

I had believed the nightmare to be over. But my meeting with Stephen, after all these years, had brought my emotions bubbling to the surface again.

My untouched breakfast was finally removed and the busy morning ward routine began. But I was no longer a part of it. There was now nothing left for me to do but wait till half past nine when the taxi would crunch to the curb outside the hospital door.

———

"How can I ever thank you?" I said to Judy as we stood together on the steps leading to the hospital. "You've been so kind."

"You don't have to," she replied, pushing me into the waiting cab.

I would have liked to have hugged her, but it wasn't in our habits; we didn't even shake hands. I just waved out the back window as she stood smiling and erect in the hospital doorway.

When the taxi drew up in front of Victoria Station, there were people with leaflets standing on the curb, and others selling flags. A middle-aged woman approached me and thrust a paper into my hands as I stepped onto the pavement.

"What is it for?" I asked, as the cab drew away.

"We're protesting against the proposed abortion laws," her companion replied, fastening a pin onto my coat.

"I see," I said bleakly, dropping my change into the proffered box. And felt a hypocrite for doing so.

Nineteen sixty-seven was the year the law legalizing abortion was passed in Britain. From the moment I left the hospital, the whole of southern England seemed to be plastered with anti- and pro-life posters, announcements of meetings, demonstrations, even discussions, all of which must have been up when I arrived. But I hadn't noticed them.

Now they glared down at me from every available space. And as the murderer is said to be drawn irresistibly back to the scene of his crime, so it was for me. In my hypersensitive, guilt-ridden state, it was almost as if I were a magnet, drawing toward myself anything that might have the remotest connection with the slaughter of an unborn baby. From newspapers, magazines, radio programs, television, and even general discussions, the word *abortion* leaped out from among all the others and dangled menacingly before my eyes.

On my way to the platform I stopped at the station book stand. Seeing that the newspaper headlines were all shrieking the dreaded word, I avoided them and haphazardly picked up a couple of women's magazines to read on the journey. But when I opened the glossy cover as the train began to draw away from the platform, there on the first page was a huge caption and underneath it the picture of a three-month-old fetus with details of how it was extracted from the womb.

I let the magazine fall from my lap and looked bleakly out the window. All the guilt I had felt, which seemed to have left me once the decision had finally been made, came pouring over me again in an icy flood, threatening to submerge me in its crashing waves. Although I didn't know it at the time, this was to be the pattern of my emotions in the ensuing months: seering guilt laced with dreadful anguish.

As the train gathered speed and rumbled past Big Ben, the Houses of Parliament, St. Thomas's Hospital, and all the old and new buildings that make up London's skyline, I sat and wept, asking myself again and again what I had done. Remorse and depression fused together with my guilt and bore down on me, screaming, tearing at my ragged nerves and threatening to drag me back once more into the pit of despair.

nine

I woke with a start as the train jerked to a standstill, and I heard the familiar sounds of carriage doors slamming and porters' carts being trundled along the platform. We had arrived at Dover. I realized as I looked out of the window and across the harbor at the steady drizzle that had begun to fall that, in spite of everything, I had slept for most of the journey.

But it wasn't a refreshing, health-giving sleep. Reaching for my case, I felt spent and lifeless and wondered whether I had, after all, been right to defy the advice of Professor Ponting and Judy, and leave.

As I walked up the gangway and onto the boat, I made for the farthest corner of the saloon and sat facing the wall, my back to the world. Most of the other passengers went straight into the restaurant. But I had never been a good sailor, and at that moment, the mere thought of food nauseated me. All I wanted was to be left alone, to sit mindlessly in my own self-made vacuum.

Shouts from the quayside and the grinding sound of

heaving ropes being slowly unwound mingled with the rising hum of the engines, and I felt the gentle sway as the boat began to draw slowly away from the harbor. I had purposefully left the magazines in the train, fearful of seeing more in their pages that could tear at my taut nerves. For want of something better to do, I took out my tapestry and settled down to while away the hour and three quarters until I would be on firm ground again.

As I rummaged among the colored wools in the pretty embroidered workbag my mother had given me, a short, middle-aged woman came and sat down on the opposite seat.

I looked up, frowning with irritation. But she ignored me and gazed pensively out the window at the activity on the harbor front, her elbow propped on the sill. The boat was gathering speed, moving smoothly over the oily, rain-drenched sea when an announcement about lunch being served came over the loudspeaker.

My companion looked over and smiled. "Do you often do this trip?" she asked pleasantly.

"Quite often," I replied, wondering how I could possibly put an end to any further conversation without being downright rude.

"So do I," she went on. "At least, since my hubby died, I've been over more often."

I panicked. I didn't want to hear anyone's life story. And

I looked desperately around for a means of escape. But there was none.

"Are you going to Paris?" she inquired.

"Yes," I replied tightly, not taking my eyes off my work as I savagely thrust the needle into the unprotesting canvas, hoping she would take the hint. But she didn't.

"We went to Paris once," she went on dreamily, "Arthur and I. I thought it was beautiful."

"It is," I answered laconically.

"I'm only going to Calais this time," she volunteered, "to bring back my son."

I kept my eyes glued to my tapestry and made no comment.

"We were supposed to come over with my mother-in-law to spend Christmas with Arthur's sister and her family. But I was rushed to the hospital with appendicitis two days before, so his gran brought Ian over on her own. But they insisted on me coming over as soon as I could to convalesce."

I put down my tapestry and looked at her. She must have been well over fifty, and I couldn't understand how she could have a son who was not old enough to cross the channel alone.

"What's your sister-in-law doing in Calais?" I asked, intrigued in spite of myself.

"Mollie married a Frenchman during the war," she

answered eagerly, having finally sparked off my interest. "Emile's a farmer outside of Calais, and Ian loves going over to stay. His cousins call him Jan," she ended with a smile.

I looked at her intently, without answering, but I think she sensed the unformed question in my mind.

"He's mentally handicapped," she said quietly.

"I see," I murmured, and added lamely, "I'm sorry."

And we sat in silence for a few minutes while I searched frantically for some words to say, something conventional.

"We always wanted a son," she continued softly. "Then when he was born it was such a shock I couldn't stop crying. But Arthur was marvelous. He took the baby in his arms and said, 'God has given me a son…and I love him.'"

She paused and propped her hand on her chin, gazing out the window at the misty outline of Dover's receding white cliffs.

"He was a wonderful father," she went on, almost to herself. "Always treated Ian as if he was normal and took him everywhere with him. It was an awful shock when he died."

"How did it happen?" I asked gently, remorseful for my past indifference.

"A very quick cancer," she said. "He'd never smoked or been much of a drinker. I just couldn't believe it."

There was a silence in which each of us tried to find words to express our feelings.

"I don't think I'd really accepted Ian till then," she mused at last.

I raised my eyebrows in surprise.

"Oh," she went on, "he was my son and I loved him,…but not like Arthur did. I think deep down I resented him for not being like other boys. But now…I don't know what I'd have done without him."

She paused again, and I saw tears in her deep-set eyes, which looked as if they had shed many in their time.

"When his dad died, Ian seemed to know what I was going through more than anyone else. He didn't say much. He's not a great talker. But he understood my feelings and moods. He never minded if I snapped his head off or was bad tempered. He just went on loving me no matter what I did. I suppose like the love of Jesus his dad talked about so much in those last few weeks before he died."

She looked up at me and smiled through her tears.

"Arthur was a Christian," she added simply. "All his family are. They've been marvelous to Ian and me since he died."

She dabbed her eyes and, embarrassed, I stared out the window to where, on the far horizon, the hump of Calais was rising out of the foam-flecked sea.

"These Christians *do* seem to have something that makes them different," she murmured, almost to herself.

Suddenly she turned and looked directly at me.

"Are *you* a Christian?" she asked abruptly.

Her question took me by surprise. And I didn't know what to reply. I had thought I was, but the past two weeks had caused me to wonder. In that instant I suddenly knew I wasn't. But I didn't want to admit it.

"I go to church," I hedged.

She nodded noncommitally.

"*Real* Christians do seem to have something special about them, don't they?" she said wistfully, obviously not equating me among them. "They have hope and peace no matter what happens."

I nodded bleakly. And for a while we sat in silence, each thinking our own thoughts.

"Did you see those people at Victoria campaigning against abortion?" she inquired at last.

My heart thundered. Then began hurling itself around my chest before flying into my throat in an attempt to block my breathing. I opened my mouth to reply, but no words came out. My companion didn't seem to notice.

"I suppose," she reflected, "if Ian had been on the way today, the doctors would have known he wasn't normal and advised me to have an abortion. And I expect I would have agreed. But just *think* what I'd have missed. Ian was such a joy to his dad. And since my hubby died, I don't think I would have carried on without him. Yet as far as the outside world is concerned, he's a reject. An article that isn't perfect."

She looked across at me appealingly, tears once again glistening in her eyes.

"Why do we have to be perfect to be accepted?" she whispered helplessly. "Some of the prettiest flowers are torn up by the roots and tossed on the rubbish heap because they are called weeds.... And now we're trying to do the same thing to unborn babies."

"I don't know," I answered, averting her gaze. "I honestly don't know."

And I wearily leaned my head against the back of the seat and closed my eyes as the overwhelming sadness of the "might-have-beens" bore down on me in a rushing tide. I think I realized then that God holds us responsible for the things we cannot see. That he never reopens doors that we have willfully shut. Doors that need never have been shut. Imaginations that need never have been tainted.

"Dear God," I silently pleaded, "am I to be spared nothing? Is my crime going to follow me everywhere I go for the rest of my life?"

There was no answer. Only a sudden lurch as the ship's engines ground to a halt.

My companion's expression changed immediately. She jumped to her feet, a smile of anticipation on her face as we walked together toward the gangplank.

Her face suddenly lit up as we waited in line at the passport control. She stood on tiptoe, waving frantically. I looked up and there on the other side of customs was a middle-aged couple with a tall, gangling youth standing between them. His face was flat and his eyes looked vacant. But as he caught sight of his mother, his whole expression changed, and the sweetest smile spread across his dull mongoloid features. He raised his arm in a joyful salute as she picked up her suitcase.

"That's Ian," she breathed, turning to me, her eyes shining. "Good-bye. Perhaps I'll bump into you again sometime."

"Perhaps." I smiled as she ran forward to be almost swept off her feet in a gigantic bear hug.

I passed the little group on my way to the waiting train. Her brother-in-law raised his cap. But she was oblivious of me as she walked away, one arm linked in her sister-in-law's and the other held tightly by the handicapped son who had turned out to be such a blessing. The child who, had she known and been given the choice, would never have been born.

Afraid that those tears that were threatening yet again would brim over, I hurried, head down, along the platform and, huddling into a corner of an empty compartment, gave myself up to remorse and self-pity.

"Mine wasn't even an imperfect specimen," I cried brokenly. Her words had dug deeply into a wound I now thought would never heal. "It's *I* who am abnormal."

The train whirred and set into motion. Through a haze

of tears I gazed bleakly out of the window at the wintry, rain-drenched landscape of northern France. But as the wheels slid rhythmically over the steel rails carrying me back to my home and my family who loved me, above the lilt of their regular click I seemed to hear a small voice pleading over and over again, "Let me live, let me live, let me live."

And once again, I broke down and wept.

ten

The fatigue and the tension of the past few weeks over-came me, and when I awoke, the flat brown countryside had vanished to be replaced by the outskirts of Paris. As the round green dome of the Abbey of St. Denis flashed by the carriage window, the monotonous rhythm of the train changed subtly and it started to reduce speed as it prepared to snake around the corner and slide into the station.

I reached for my case and, struggling to get my coat, looked anxiously out the carriage window as, exactly on time, the train drew into Gare du Nord. Although the boat had appeared to be half empty, there was a mass of people milling about on the platform waiting for the passengers to alight, and I couldn't see Jacques over the heads of the crowd. Climbing down slowly from the high step, I started to walk toward the barrier, my eyes scanning the distance. As the travelers began to disperse, I caught sight of him walking up the platform, his eyes anxiously peering through the advancing passengers.

Christopher was perched in the crook of his arm and

his free hand held tightly to Yves, who was walking purposefully at his side, his eyes darting like lizards in every direction. Yves was wearing a pair of muddy Wellingtons on the wrong feet and Bee's rather grubby Isle of Arran sweater, which was far too big for him and hung somewhere round his knees. I half expected to see Bee with her Tongan nose flute bringing up the rear, then remembered it was Friday, and she would be at her ballet lesson.

Suddenly Yves caught sight of me and, breaking away from his father's grasp, lolloped down the platform toward me, his progress somewhat hampered by his unusual footwear. I dropped my case and, kneeling on the dirty concrete, held out my arms.

He rushed into them and snuggled up contentedly as I held him close, pouring kisses on his lank blond hair, which smelled unpleasantly of fish. In fact, his whole small person seemed to smell of something undefinable. I decided that the trip to the lake the previous Saturday had obviously been a success.

Jacques came up behind him, a broad smile on his face, and, stooping, bent Christopher in my direction for him to kiss me. But my little son turned his face away and buried his golden curls in his father's shoulder.

"Don't worry," soothed my husband as he picked up my case. "He probably needs time to get used to you again."

He glanced at Yves who was swinging delightedly from

my hand. "I'm afraid he's not 100 percent clean and tidy," he mentioned apologetically.

That was the understatement of the year! I nodded absently as we began to walk toward the barrier, Yves's nonstop chatter covering any awkwardness the situation might have produced. I looked across at my younger son, annoyed with myself for being affected by his attitude. But his chubby little face was turned determinedly away from me, firmly hidden in his father's shoulder.

As I got into the car Jacques dumped Christopher on my knee. I put my arms around him to cuddle him close but he sat bolt upright and deliberately turned his head away.

"Take no notice," said my husband comfortingly. "He'll be all right in a while."

But my fragile nerves were already sending out signals to each other as I realized that Christopher had rejected me. It was only to be expected, I told myself.

How many times in his short life had he woken up to discover that his mother wasn't there? I thought back. He was only six months old when I had my breakdown. Jacques had occasionally brought him to the clinic on a fine Saturday afternoon and plonked him down on the grass beside me in that lovely garden where with the other patients I spent most of my days that beautiful summer, cut off from the outside world, locked in an icy loneliness. But he couldn't have understood very much of what was going on. And then, when he did get me back and got used to having me around, just after his first birthday, I had mysteriously disappeared again, and this time he didn't come to visit me. It was November and I was mostly in my room, and Jacques had obviously thought it better not to subject him to that.

I glanced at my husband as he weaved in and out of traffic, which was gradually piling up around us as the rush hour closed in, and felt a wave of tenderness. It couldn't have been easy for him having a wife who had been depressed and half crazy ever since she came home from the hospital with the adorable child who was now sitting stiffly on her knee gazing straight in front of him. But Jacques had never complained, just had taken everything in his stride. And I knew that he had something that I didn't, something that money could not buy. That "something" my companion on the boat had talked about and that her Arthur had possessed.

We both went to church. We both had been very much involved in church activities. But Jacques had that something extra that I had noticed before in some people but couldn't quite define what it was. A rare tranquillity that dominated every situation and carried him over each successive wave as it was about to crash down on his head and suck him into the depths. And I knew it had to do with his "conversion." With the fact that his Bible was more than a dusty book on a shelf. It was instead a manual he read daily, with which he was familiar and which he couldn't do without.

He had left me a copy of the New Testament the first time I was in the clinic, and I had dutifully read a chapter each evening but it had not meant very much, and the habit had since lapsed. I sighed and Jacques looked up at me through the driving mirror and smiled.

"Won't be long now," he comforted, mistaking my sigh for impatience at the stop-start progress we were making. "Once we get out of Paris and on to the motorway, we'll be home in no time."

"Oh, it's all right," I answered. "I was just thinking it can't have been easy for you all these months, me being such a wet blanket."

He smiled again.

"Don't suppose it was very easy for you, either," he said quietly. "But we've managed. And now I'm sure everything is going to be all right."

Jacques was always optimistic. I hoped so. But I was far from sure.

Yves's chatter had begun to trail off, and as we finally drove across the St. Cloud Bridge and on to the motorway, he snuggled up next to me and his eyes closed. I put my arm around him and drew him close, and as I did so, I was aware that Christopher had changed his position slightly. His violet-blue eyes were gazing at me as if sizing me up.

Dare he trust me? Would I let him down again if he

allowed himself to be drawn back into that warm web of affection from which he had been snatched so many times?

Yves sighed deeply in his sleep. I looked at Christopher and smiled, not daring to move or take the initiative. Suddenly he leaned toward me and, as my free arm closed around him, snuggled closer and wriggled himself into position until he was cradled in my arm.

I bent my head and buried my face in his soft golden curls. He looked up, and I kissed the warm, rosy cheek as, with a sigh, he too cuddled closer and closed his eyes.

I saw Jacques glance at us through the driving mirror. He gave a conspiratorial wink and turned off the motorway and down the hill to the horse pond at the entrance to our village.

We were home again.

There was the noisy pandemonium of dogs excitedly barking as they heard the car stop before the front door, which was immediately flung open, and Bee appeared, her face wreathed in smiles. She wrenched open the back door of the car and both boys woke up abruptly but, strangely enough, didn't cry. Yves yawned, stretched, and fell out of the car. Christopher blinked, then snuggled down again. I climbed out with him still in my arms as a cloud of dogs burst upon us, and Bee jumped up and down excitedly, demanding to know if I'd remembered to buy her Smarties.

I smiled and tweaked her nose.

I was home again. I was safe. Everything was going to be all right.

Or so I thought.

eleven

As if to confirm my intuition, the weekend was perfect. The changeable weather I had encountered in England and the rain that swept through the Pas de Calais seemed to have glided over Paris, and there was even a hint of spring in the air when I awoke that Saturday morning.

Christopher waddled into our bedroom, warm and cuddly, and climbed in beside me, sucking contentedly on the strip of his blanket that he'd insisted on having in his crib ever since my first "disappearance." He smiled up at me as he nestled closer. Yves, on the surface, didn't appear to have been at all affected by my absence, and everything just slipped back into the normal bustle. The other three didn't even seem to have noticed that I'd left and, apart from the fact that her bosom friend had given Bee a pair of premature chickens that she had tried unsuccessfully to raise in her bedroom with dire and extremely smelly results, the surface of our family life didn't appear even to have been ruffled.

The break from routine and responsibilities, despite

the reason, had done me good, and I took up the reins again, glad, for the moment, to be home.

Professor Ponting had prescribed some medication to tide me over till I could consult my own doctor, and after those weeks of tension and anguish, the future now appeared settled. I deliberately put the conversation with Stephen out of my mind and convinced myself that I had turned the page and everything would once again return to normal. It's amazing the "illusions" drugs can create. And that is exactly what they were doing for me, perhaps mercifully, that bright January weekend.

I saw Dr. Dufour, without great enthusiasm, on the following Monday afternoon, but it was more to please Jacques than anything else. Although he had treated me after Christopher's birth when I had sunk into that bleak postnatal depression, I hadn't had confidence in him then, and since my two stays in the clinic, in my opinion, proved to be total failures, my faith in him had rapidly disappeared. But I had promised Judy I would see the psychiatrist when I got back, so dutifully went along. As I expected, he put me back on the drugs I had been popping endlessly over the past few months. He asked me to come back in two weeks, and I mentally added, "We'll see." As it happened, I was never to set eyes on him again.

On the Thursday evening after my return, Jacques tentatively mentioned that he really ought to leave for two or three days the following week, and anxiously asked me if I thought I could cope. I laughed at him.

"Of *course* I can cope," I replied. "Whatever made you think I couldn't?"

"I didn't think you *couldn't*," he soothed. "It's just that…"

"You wondered whether I'd jump out the window, possibly taking the children along with me," I cut in dryly.

He sat down on the sofa beside me.

"No," he said gently, "it's not that. But you've been through a bad time, and if you don't feel up to being on your own I can put off my trip for a week or two."

"I'll hardly be on my own with five children around," I answered exasperatedly, hating myself for my abruptness. Why did I want to hurt people all the time, especially Jacques, who was kindness itself and who had already put up with more than enough?

But as usual, he appeared not to even notice my irritation.

"That's just it," he went on. "Five children is quite a load."

I said nothing, that feeling of guilt once again sweeping over me. Other women managed on their own with five children, why did he think I couldn't? But Jacques must have sensed my thoughts.

"Of course you can cope," he said soothingly. "But you've just had an operation. Anyway, if you're not feeling too tired, I'll leave on Monday and be back on Thursday or

Friday." He made a rueful face. "More likely to be Friday, I'm afraid."

He disliked traveling as much as most men whose heart is really at home with their family. I smiled, sorry for my bad temper.

"Don't worry," I said, full of remorse. "There's no problem, just stay away as long as you need to, everything will be fine here. The children seem to be going through an 'angelic' phase." And I laughed.

"Didn't know such a stage existed," Jacques said. "Doesn't say anything about it in the books; they usually hint darkly at just the opposite."

"Maybe we've discovered a new formula for child raising," I added. "Perhaps I should write and sell the idea to Dr. Spock."

This time we both laughed. Dr. Spock was currently my hero, and his method my bible.

I was still feeling that I could cope when Jacques left on Monday morning. He called me from the office in the late afternoon before taking his plane and went off reassured. I was reassured too and got up on Tuesday, planning things I would do during my few days of enforced freedom. Then the telephone rang.

"So you're back," Jenny's laughing voice came on the line. "I called last week and one of the boys said you were in England. Did you have a good time?"

"It was a change," I answered cryptically.

"Nice to have a change this time of year," she went on brightly. "Everything seems so flat after Christmas."

"How are you feeling now?" Her voice was concerned. She was one of those faithful friends who had written to me and supported me in prayer during my stays in the clinic.

"I'm very well," I answered truthfully. "It's all behind me now."

And I sincerely thought it was.

"I'm so pleased," Jenny continued warmly. "We've missed you these last few months."

"Thank you," I answered lamely, not knowing what else to say.

There was a pause and I felt that she hadn't finished. That there was something she wanted to tell me but was not quite sure how to get it out.

"Have you heard our news?" she volunteered finally.

"No," I puzzled. "What news?"

"We're expecting an addition to our family," she announced.

My heart missed a beat and for a second seemed to stop beating altogether. Then it shot up into my throat as it had done on the boat and prevented me from speaking. There was an awkward silence during which time the line crackled.

"Hallo," Jenny called anxiously. "Are you still there?"

"Yes," I managed to gasp.

"Didn't mean to give you such a shock," she said with genuine concern in her voice.

I managed a slight laugh to reassure her. "It's not a shock," I replied. "Just…rather unexpected."

Jenny laughed, breaking the tension.

"Not nearly so much as it was to us," she said brightly, and I couldn't understand the gaiety in her voice, after her initial announcement. She was only a few years younger than I and already had four children, all of them in school. Apart from anything else, she and David had finally realized their ambition to move out of Paris and build their dream house farther into the country than we were. The house was lovely, set in two acres of land, but I knew it had been an uphill struggle financially and would continue to be so for some years to come. Jenny had told me that vacations had been sacrificed because of it, and she had sometimes wondered whether, as far as the children were concerned, it had been right. But they all seemed very happy in their new home, and Jenny, who adored gardening, was in her element.

"It's wonderful news," I volunteered at last. "But how do you feel about it?"

"Now?" she went on. "Oh, now it's fine. I'm at the end of my dreaded three months and coming up on the good period."

Jenny had always had terrible morning sickness in the early days of her pregnancies with the other four, and the pattern had obviously repeated itself.

"Yes, but mentally," I urged. "Apart from the sickness."

"Oh, mentally," she replied, "no problem at all now we've gotten over the initial shock. And Caroline is delighted. She's always held it against me for giving her three brothers, so now she's over the moon, knitting pink bootees for the long-awaited little sister."

Jenny laughed again. But that was Jenny. She always laughed. "Only hope I don't let her down," she ended.

"But isn't it going to be a bit difficult for you financially?" I asked. "I know only too well what plunging into house-buying means."

"Well," Jenny replied thoughtfully, "we could have done without another. But by the time he or she, better say *she* and be positive for Caroline's sake, starts wanting to be educated, let's hope the worst will be over. And anyway," she ended confidently, "the Lord will provide.... He always does."

I said nothing. But, marveling at her assurance and her faith, it suddenly crossed my mind that if I had had her radiant faith, maybe he would have provided for me, too. And for a split second, I threatened to somber once again into guilt and despair. Then I quickly pulled myself together. For me it was different. But was it? That small, inner voice nagged, and that unspoken question in Stephen's eyes danced sadly before me. Jenny's voice broke in on my brooding.

"Have you heard from Lucille?" she inquired.

"No," I answered, seeming to come back from a long way. "I've been so busy since I got back I've hardly had time to call anyone."

"Oh," Jenny said cryptically. "So you don't know her news either?"

"No," I hedged.

"She's joined the club," Jenny pealed. "Her baby is due three days before mine."

"What?" I gasped.

"Yes," Jenny continued joyfully. "Unbelievable, isn't it? Lucille, always so organized and methodical and now this has happened. Shows you can never be sure of anything in this world, doesn't it? It's like an epidemic at the moment. You'd better be careful you don't catch the bug."

Once again my heart seemed to stand still and then clutch at my throat. Jenny took my silence for astonishment.

"Look," she went on, "why don't you come and have tea? It would be lovely to see you again. I promised Jacques some cuttings from my alpines, and that'll save me climbing out of my garden boots and bringing them over. Today any use to you?"

I bit my lip.

"Jenny," I stammered, "could I call you back? Jacques is away at the moment and I'm not organized. Perhaps not today, but one afternoon this week. I'll give you a call."

"Lovely," Jenny replied. "I'm not moving; just give me time to rush in from the garden when you call, won't you?"

And we hung up.

I sat down heavily on the window seat in the hall, all sorts of thoughts racing crazily around and around in my mind. Jenny I could understand. She was sweet and feminine and motherly and another baby would always be welcome in that home, even if it did mean tightening their belts. But Lucille? I picked up the phone to dial her number. It was busy. I wasn't surprised; her phone was always busy. Lucille was the busiest, most organized woman I had ever known. In fact, just to think about what she got done in a week made me tired.

I tried again, but the short, sharp ring announced that Lucille was still talking.

Her name didn't suit her in the least. For me it was the very essence of femininity, conjuring up pictures of parasols and floppy hats dripping with ribbons and rosebuds and billowing chiffon gowns. But Lucille Dillon was the no-nonsense type. Plain and practical, she appeared to make no effort to improve herself. Her face was devoid of makeup, her mousy hair scraped back into an uncompromising bun, and her clothes were good but sensible. She had earned a high-powered scientific degree at one of the older universities and had been teaching mathematics to sixth graders when she and Lionel married. I never understood why they did marry. They seemed totally unsuited.

He was a soft-spoken, handsome man whose innate courtesy contrasted sharply with Lucille's abruptness. But they appeared to be blissfully happy, and since their three superintelligent children had begun school in earnest, Lucille had thrown herself wholeheartedly into helping Lionel, who had just set up a law practice on his own account, albeit with slight trepidation on his part but great determination on hers.

This sinking of their funds meant they had been unable to move from their small flat. But since their children were all bookworms immersed in their studies and not very interested in sports, the lack of room didn't then present a problem. But now, where on earth would they put a baby? I wondered. There simply wasn't even cupboard space available. And how would Lionel manage without Lucille's confident help?

I picked up the phone and dialed again.

"Hello," came Lucille's voice. It was surprisingly young, soft and modulated, contrasting sharply with her stern appearance and the brusque words it frequently uttered. When people met her for the first time, they were often astonished at the difference between the voice and the owner.

"Lucille," I answered. "I've just been talking with Jenny and she told me your wonderful news. I'm ringing to ask you how you feel."

"Emotionally or physically?" she answered practically.

"Both," I replied.

"Well, physically, no problem," she went on. "Mentally…well, it has taken a little time to get used to the idea, but it's finally sunk in and no problem now. And you, how are you feeling after all this time?"

It had been a long time. I felt I had been out of circulation for so long that all my friends could now be pushing new babies in buggies without my even having heard about it.

"Oh, I'm fine," I replied.

"Good."

Lucille never wasted words.

"And Lionel?" I pursued. "How's the practice going?"

"Slow to get off the ground," Lucille replied. "But it's coming along, it's coming. We didn't expect it to fly off right from the start. Lionel gave himself five years and we've still another two to go."

"Will a new baby be a great handicap?" I ventured.

"Well," she replied, "it certainly won't be a help. But we'll manage. I think Lionel is even pleased."

"I didn't know whether to congratulate or commiserate," I went on.

"Oh, don't commiserate," Lucille said briskly. "Must be positive. What happened has happened and that's all there is to it."

I wished for a moment that I could be like her.

"Had a sticky time telling my parents," she continued. That remark took me completely by surprise. I had somehow never thought of Lucille as having parents. I had met Lionel's mother when she was here on a visit, but Lucille had always appeared so self-reliant, I couldn't even imagine her ever having been a child and must have thought that, like Topsy, "she just growed."

"What did they say?" I asked.

"Oh, we just took the bull by the horns when we knew and called them. Told them it was a mistake and they took it very well."

Again something clutched at my heart. A mistake. How could a little baby, a growing human life, ever be considered a "mistake"?

"I'm so glad," I answered lamely, not knowing what else to say.

"We're adjusted to the idea now," she went on. "Just a question of getting organized."

Dear Lucille, she would cope. Organization was her key word.

"I'm going over to tea with Jenny one afternoon this week," I went on. "Why don't you come too?"

I had never understood the friendship between Lucille and Jenny. They were so very different. But then I hadn't understood her marriage to Lionel, either. And I came to the conclusion that there were obviously a lot of things I didn't understand.

"My dear, I'd love to come," Lucille went on, "but this week is out, I'm afraid."

"More committees?" I teased.

She laughed. That was one good thing about Lucille, she never minded a joke against herself.

"Well, I have cut down drastically since I began helping Lionel."

"But are still on far more than any normal woman could cope with?" I teased.

"Not quite," she replied. "And with number four coming along, I suppose I'll curtail even further. But I'm arranging to do a lot of the work from home."

"Dear Lucille," I said, "you make me feel tired just thinking of the amount of things you manage to gallop through in a day."

"Nonsense," she replied, but obviously pleased at the compliment. "We all have our gifts, don't we?"

And I remembered the day I had called to collect her for a "do" at the embassy and found her still in slacks talking on the phone.

"With you in three minutes," she had called putting down the receiver and making for the bathroom.

I had flopped down on the sofa in dismay, convinced that we would be hopelessly late, but true to her word, she was ready in three minutes flat.

"Wouldn't make any difference to the way I look however long I spent doing myself up, so there's no point in wasting time trying, is there?" she had stated as she joined me.

Now, thinking back, I wondered if Lucille didn't have a complex about being so plain and whether she needed all this outside committee work to bolster her inner fears. And I saw my friend in a new light.

"You certainly have more gifts than most of us," I said quietly. "What would we do without you?"

Lucille gave an awkward cough, and I knew that I had embarrassed her.

"Must go, my dear," she said abruptly. "Give my love to Jenny. See you very soon, I hope."

And she put down the receiver. I sat staring at nothing in particular, incapable of making head or tail of my matted thoughts.

It had been a bombshell to learn that Jenny was expecting another baby. But when I heard that Lucille was also to become a mother again, the knife that had been precariously poised over the wound in my heart now slowly dropped and began to grind insidiously around and around. They were both three months pregnant, as I had so recently been.

I bit my lip as tears of regret and self-pity began to prick my eyes.

This autumn my two friends would both be going to the church meetings, swinging babies in infant carriers.

As this thought crossed my mind, the threatened tears receded and I smiled, feeling sure that Lucille would dig her ancient pram out of the cellar for the new baby. She had pushed that creaking structure around the park with the other three, scorning the astonished looks of passersby, saying that it didn't matter to the baby what sort of pram it had or whether the sheets were embroidered or not, so why waste money on such frivolities. And Jenny would look radiant and happy and laugh and trust the Lord to provide. And I couldn't help wondering what my reaction would have been.

"Probably the asylum," I muttered bitterly, and tried to put the thought from me.

But it wouldn't go away.

I went into the kitchen to prepare the boys' lunch, and a great wave of bitterness and self-pity washed over me. Would I ever be on my feet again? I wondered angrily. I had believed I was, and then this double bombshell this morning seemed to have shattered my fragile peace. I switched on the radio to take my thoughts off myself. There were three pips and time for the news.

"There have been angry demonstrations in London," came the announcer's smooth tones, "over the proposed abortion laws."

With a fierce gesture I switched it off.

Was I never going to have any peace? Was that dreaded word and its consequences going to haunt me? No, more than haunt me, flatten over me like a heavy net, and there didn't seem to be any way of escape. In my heart I knew there was no escape. No escape from this searing guilt that, after my few days of false euphoria when I had believed that everything was all right again, had risen to the surface and was leering at me with its snake's mouth open, waiting to strike.

Without thinking, I looked up at the calendar hanging on the kitchen wall. Jenny had sent it to me at Christmas time and there was a Bible quotation for each day. I read "Be strong and of a good courage; be not afraid, neither be thou dismayed: for the Lord thy God is with thee whithersoever thou goest" (Joshua 1:9). Those words struck my heart at that moment as being just for me. I was afraid; afraid of the future, afraid of going back into that psychiatric clinic, yet afraid of not being able to cope without it; afraid of the medication I was taking that I knew would have to be increased and increased as my fears and my anguish mounted. I had no courage and I was dismayed. Yet that verse said that God was with me wherever I went. Dare I believe it?

And once again those words I had heard in that little Essex church two Sundays previously, and which also seemed to have been chosen especially for me, crept back into my mind: "Thou wilt keep him in perfect peace, whose mind is stayed on thee: because he trusteth in thee."

That was what Jenny was doing. She trusted in the Lord. He filled her whole life, her every waking thought. She was radiant with love. Even now, in the difficult early months of her unexpected pregnancy, with all the financial burdens this new baby implied, he had given her his peace. She had taken his words to heart, she was not dismayed, she was not worried because she knew, she had that wonderful blessed assurance that the Lord, her God and Jacques' God, would be with her wherever she went.

And I knew that he could be my God too. That he had revealed himself to me in that little Norman church. And I realized, at that moment, that I had been praying empty prayers all those years. I had been dutifully attending church and reciting meaningless phrases every Sunday. Meaningless to me. And I knew that my God was not her God. Her God, her Lord, her Father, as she called him was real, helping her, encouraging her, supporting her, loving her…and mine was not. And I wanted to know why.

Walking slowly back into the hall I picked up the phone. Jenny's voice came on the line.

"Jenny," I said breathlessly, "I've changed my mind. I'd like to come to tea this afternoon."

"Oh, lovely," she said.

"It doesn't matter about the cuttings," I went on hurriedly, fearing she might suddenly remember the reason for my visit and change the day. "I can pick them up some other time."

"Oh, there's no problem," she answered. "I can go get them now. I've no one home for lunch…or the moment."

A smell of burning wafting from the kitchen reminded me of the vegetables bubbling on the stove.

"But I *have*," I echoed, feeling suddenly light and joyful.

"See you about three?" she asked. "Claire's just rung, and she's popping in this afternoon too; she'll be so pleased you're coming, she often asks after you. You remember her, don't you? She and Quentin came to the barbecue we had last summer when we finally moved into the house."

"Yes, I remember," I said slowly, "but I must rush; everything is burning dry."

"I know the feeling," Jenny groaned. "Off you go."

And she hung up.

I ran into the kitchen and rescued the carrots before they were at disaster point. I felt a little flat all of a sudden. I'd rather hoped to see Jenny on her own. I don't know what I intended to say to her, or ask her, but I'd wanted it to be just the two of us, and now Claire was going to be there. For a split second I considered calling Jenny back and saying I'd come another day. Then I realized how ridiculous the situation would be. I'd already said I wasn't free this afternoon, then called to say I was. I couldn't, in all sanity, call again five minutes later and say that after all I wasn't. So I let the matter drop.

I'd met Claire; she was another member of Jenny's "God-squad," an affectionate name applied to those committed Christians in our group by us "good churchgoers." They had a radiance, a special quality about them we secretly envied but didn't particularly want to take the trouble to acquire. It meant calling God Father and Lord, being on a chummy basis with Jesus. Attending prayer meetings and Bible studies, which were very time-consuming and not particularly interesting, besides being highly embarrassing at times. They sang choruses!

"Oh well," I said philosophically as I heard Christopher stirring from his nap and jabbering incomprehensibly to himself, it'll make a change to go out and be back in circulation again. Even if the circulation could prove dangerous.

And I laughed. But it was a hollow sound, a mocking sound. Very different from Jenny's gay trill. That black cloud was hovering above me, and I knew it would not be long before it came down and smothered me again.

By the time I had come back down into the kitchen with Christopher in my arms, it had done so and was sitting heavily on my head, stifling me, shutting out all light. And I knew that the past few days of normality had been a reprieve, and now the darkness was back for good.

"I can't bear it," I choked. "I can't take it anymore."

I heard a car draw up outside the house, then a door slam and the clatter of Yves' footsteps in the hall. His shout of "Mummie" came to me as through a thick, dark cloud through which I could see neither to the right or left, as he burst into the kitchen and rushed up behind me grabbing the back of my knees.

"Don't *do* that," I shouted, and he backed away, fear in his big blue eyes.

Christopher looked up from his high chair and began to cry. I didn't know why I had reacted so strongly and I went to take Yves in my arms. But he put his hands up in front of his face as if to ward me off and slithered over to where Christopher was wailing in his high chair, squeezing himself into the corner, away from my grasp.

I turned back to the stove and began furiously mashing carrots and potatoes, tears streaming down my face. I felt a failure as a wife, as a mother, as a woman. As I admitted my utter worthlessness, that leering snake smiled and retreated, leaving the heavy black cloud and the thick gray fog all around me.

I didn't go to Jenny's. I just sat in a blank stupor while Christopher played uncomplaining around my feet. Yves didn't usually go to school in the afternoon, but he had elected to do so that day. I decided he was glad to be away from me, and that only increased my guilt and misery.

By the time Jacqeus came home on Thursday evening, he must have sensed the deadness in my voice when he rang the day before and cut short his trip—I was back on the merry-go-round again. Half crazy with depression. Feeling completely unable to cope.

On Saturday morning, in desperation, Jacques rang Dr. Dufour, who said the only thing to do was to readmit me to the clinic. This threat roused me. For nothing in the world was I going to set foot in that place again! But I didn't want to stay at home, either. I was at peace nowhere. Life was just a long, black tunnel filled with guilt and despair, and there seemed to be no light anywhere…and no escape.

Then, on Sunday afternoon when Jacques was out walking the dogs and the children in the forest, Jenny called with a proposition.

twelve

I saw you in church this morning," she began. This time her voice didn't have that lilt of laughter. "And my fears were confirmed."

"What fears?" I asked blankly.

"The fears that started when you didn't come to tea last Tuesday."

"I couldn't make it after all," I answered bleakly. "I'm sorry, I did call...."

"I know you did," she cut in. "It's not that. It's just that...oh, we've been so concerned about you for so long. We've been praying...yet you don't seem to get any better."

I didn't answer.

"When Claire came round on Tuesday, we decided to really seek the Lord and try to find his answer to your problem."

I still made no reply. It was all so remote, so far above me. I was convinced that nothing and no one could help me and yet...could there be a ray of hope here? And I remembered the words I had heard in church only three Sundays ago.

"And did you find one?" I asked dryly.

"I think so," she replied quietly. "Could we come and talk to you about it?"

"We?" I queried, thinking she meant her husband. She and David were both radiant Christians.

"Claire and I," she ended.

"I don't know…" I began.

"We'll be round in half an hour." And she hung up.

The last thing I wanted was to be preached at. But Jenny and Claire did not preach. They sat lovingly with me, and as if they were talking to another member of the tea party, they just held me before the Lord and asked him to put his healing hands on me and bless me and take away this terrible blackness.

And, oddly enough, I was not embarrassed.

"What a pity Lucille's away this weekend," Jenny said when they had finished praying. "She would have loved to have been here."

"*Lucille?*" I queried.

"Yes." Jenny smiled. "Lucille. My, you have been out of things, haven't you?"

"But what has Lucille got to do with it?" I asked.

"Just that she's been praying for you, and she was with Claire and me last Friday morning when we had that defi-nite feeling that Jesus was very near to coming into your life. It was then he made it clear to Claire that if only you would trust him, he would deliver you from all your fears."

I was stunned. The very words that I had read on the calendar had come back to me again, in my darkest moment, through Claire's mouth. "Be not afraid, neither be thou dismayed: for the Lord thy God is with thee whithersoever thou goest." But I was intrigued about Lucille. Like me, she had always been a faithful churchgoer, on all the committees, a great worker, in fact. But I couldn't imagine her singing choruses and lifting holy hands, calling God "Father."

Jenny read my thoughts.

"It took an unexpected pregnancy to bring Lucille to Jesus," she said quietly, "just as it's taking this terrible depression to bring you."

I said nothing. I even felt rather cross that she should be so presumptuous.

"Lucille was really shattered by the news of this baby," Jenny went on. "It wasn't until she came to accept Jesus as her personal Savior and put the problem in his hands that she was able to come to terms with it."

"She seems to have come to terms with it now," I remarked dryly, seeing the seesaw position she and I were in: Lucille having come to terms with having a baby and me unable to come to terms with not having one.

"Very much so," Jenny went on. "She's even looking forward to it and has such peace of mind about the problems involved. And Lionel's really pleased."

"So she told me," I replied.

And I looked desperately at Jenny, longing to tell her why I had fallen back into this pit of despair. How her thickening waistline and tell-tale roundness plunged me into an abyss of remorse and self-pity. It would have been such a relief to come out into the open with these dear friends. But something held me back. That pride that refused to let them see the depth of my vulnerability. My hurt, my overriding feeling of inadequacy. That terrible fear of condemnation, which was so unreasonable. Everywhere I had met with nothing but love and understanding. I knew that Jenny and Claire would be the last people to judge or condemn me.

I opened my mouth to blurt out my guilty secret. But no words came. The moment passed, and I closed my lips tightly in a bitter line.

Jenny, David, and Lionel all shared Jacques' deep faith, but it seemed that Lucille and I needed a raging crisis in our lives before we were able to hand over ours.

I wasn't sure that I was ready to do so, but there was nowhere else to turn, and I felt trapped.

"What do you want me to do?" I whispered.

Jenny looked at Claire, and she came over to me and knelt on the floor, taking both my hands gently in hers.

"Just trust," she said quietly. "The medication isn't helping you much, is it?"

I shook my head dumbly, the bitterness now giving way to grief and despair.

"Then why don't you try giving it up and trusting Jesus to bring you out of the dark pit?"

I withdrew my hands in horror and looked down at her.

"Give up my medication?"

I was half crazy *with* it. Goodness only knows how I would be *without* it. But Claire sat quietly on the floor, looking up at me, her deep gray eyes full of compassion. They were wide set with thick, curling lashes and, at that moment, seemed to fill her small oval face. I hadn't noticed when I met her before how beautiful she was and how serene. And I was momentarily shocked to share such intimacy with someone I scarcely knew. Then I remembered what Jenny had said, that she had been praying for me. And I marveled afresh at the faith, the love, the dedication of these born-again Christians. Overwhelmed that Claire could spare time to pray for a mere acquaintance, someone she had only met once in a crowd at Jenny's barbecue party. And I relaxed and smiled down at her.

Claire took my hands again.

"Won't you give Jesus a chance?" she pleaded. "We had the strong conviction when we were praying for you on Friday morning that that is what he wants you to do. Throw away the crutches and lean on him—on his everlasting arms," she ended softly.

I swallowed hard but did not reply.

At that moment the door burst open and Yves fell into the sitting room. He stopped short, seeing this unusual tableau on the carpet. Jacques peered over his head and came into the room, a broad smile on his face.

"How nice of you to come," he greeted them warmly, looking inquiringly at Jenny. He guessed that this was not a purely social visit.

"Run and ask Bee to give you and Christopher your gouter," he said to Yves, mentioning the teatime snack French children always have in the afternoon.

And he sat down on the sofa beside me.

For a moment no one spoke. But the silence wasn't awkward.

"They think I should give up my drugs," I whispered at last.

My husband looked startled.

"We feel that this is what Jesus is asking her to do," Jenny said quietly. "That he wants to heal her but, so far, hasn't been able to."

Jacques looked anxiously at me and said nothing.

He alone knew that the abortion had plunged me right back to square one. That the guilt I now felt was more terrible than the black depression that had scarcely left me during the past fifteen months.

There was a current of electricity hovering in the air as

no one spoke, and each waited for the other to say the words that would snap the tension. I was hoping desperately that Jacques would, as usual, take the responsibility out of my hands, make the decision for me by saying that such a drastic step was out of the question.

Yet at the same time, another part of me, a small secret well I had not yet tapped, hoped that he wouldn't. That he would uphold me, even encourage me to abandon all to his God. But he said nothing. Just sat staring into the fire. And I knew that this was a decision only I could make. The time had arrived for me to come down on one side of the fence or the other.

I looked up, forcing him to meet my gaze, and he smiled. Then my resolve collapsed.

"I...can't," I choked in a half whisper.

Jenny and Claire said nothing.

Jacques reached across and took my hand. "Does it have to be immediately?" he asked.

Jenny bit her lip and Claire didn't reply. But it was obvious that they had come holding out to me the promise Jesus had made to them a few days before. And that the promise, once refused, might never be renewed, or at least not in the same way again.

"Perhaps," Jacques ventured, "if we left it till the weekend when I would be at home and..." his voice trailed off, not daring to put into words the fears that were uppermost in his mind. But we all knew what he was thinking. I dropped my eyes as the tears of guilt and self-hatred threatened to overflow and cascade down my cheeks.

Jenny and Claire got up and, coming over to the sofa, bent down to kiss me.

"We'll leave you," Jenny said, gently squeezing my shoulder. "But we'll be praying for you every day."

Jacques rose to accompany them to the door. I remained staring into the fire as the wretched tears broke in a torrent and great sobs shook my body and tore through me like a torrent washing away in their overwhelming tide all feeling, negative or positive, good or bad, just leaving a vast expanse of arid desert in their wake.

When Jacques came back into the room, we didn't discuss what had happened. In fact, we didn't discuss anything. For the rest of the evening we almost seemed to avoid each other, trying to stifle the burning question to which there seemed to be no sensible answer. Each of us afraid to say what was uppermost in our minds.

The following morning, the weather finally broke and winter tore down in a howling gale, lashing the house and garden with great sodden gusts that sent the children scurrying down the steps, hanging grimly onto their woolly caps, mackintoshes tightly buttoned up under their chins.

As I stood staring bleakly through the hall window at the bare, swaying trees, watching the rain, my back firmly turned to the usual Monday chaos, those words on the calendar sprang in large, black letters before my eyes and danced against the rattling window pane. "Be strong and of a good courage; be not afraid, neither be thou dismayed: for the Lord thy God is with thee whithersoever thou goest." The lines ran across the pane and vanished, blending into the great drops of rain, and the last words of the text I had heard in that little Essex church took their place: "Trust ye in the Lord for ever: for in the Lord Jehovah is everlasting strength."

I remained standing there, gazing at the window pane, but only clusters of raindrops ran ceaselessly down it. The words had gone, but their impact had not. As I turned back into the room, the dichotomy in my brain that had been driving me slowly crazy all these past months suddenly clicked into position, and I knew what I had to do.

Christopher was sitting happily in the middle of the kitchen floor, a wooden spoon in his hand, a small saucepan on his head, the contents of the cupboards strewn around him as he played delightedly amongst the debris. He had been up since six and was always happy to go back to bed for a nap midmorning—but nine o'clock was hardly midmorning. Nevertheless, I picked him up and carried him upstairs to the nursery. He settled himself comfortably in his crib, chewing contentedly on his blanket, and my heart melted as I bent to kiss his warm, soft cheek. He was such an easy baby. Such a joy. As these thoughts came into my mind, I realized that the miracle had happened. I was actually beginning to be positive. To enjoy my baby and see life in a light that wasn't perpetually shrouded in a thick, gray fog.

I closed the door softly behind me, hearing his incomprehensible mumblings as I went purposefully to the bathroom. Opening the door of the medicine cupboard, I caught a sight of myself in its mirror and was shocked at the haggard appearance. My eyes were circled in black, my mouth drooping at the corners. There was no joy, no contentment on my face. My expression was hard and bitter. What had happened to the carefree, laughing girl I had once been? The one who had been "such fun" as a probationer nurse?

Perhaps this shock was the catalyst that strengthened my resolve. Taking down boxes of wildly expensive drugs from the shelves, I walked steadily across the room and emptied them one by one into the toilet and watched the pink, blue, and white capsules swirl round and finally disappear as I flushed them down. Picking up the empty cartons, I stuffed them into the bathroom trash and went purposefully out of the room, closing the door firmly behind me.

But once outside I leaned against it, my breath coming in short gasps as the full realization of what I had done swept over me. I had thrown away my crutch. My life belt. My only support. And was now relying totally on something or someone in whom I wasn't even sure existed. As my nails bit deeply into the palms of my hands, my teeth ground remorselessly in an attempt to curb my fears and prevent them from rising up into my throat and choking me. Those words "Be strong and of a good courage; be not afraid, neither be thou dismayed: for the Lord thy God is with thee whithersoever thou goest" once again sprang up in front of my eyes and, as if on a computer screen, flashed into place, jerked across the screen, and were gone. But the effect was enough to pull me together as I ran into my bedroom and flung myself on the unmade bed crying, "Will you be with me wherever I go? Will you, God?"

There was no reply, only the low moan of the wind and rain smattering on the window panes. But I don't think I had expected one.

"Lord," I cried desperately. "I want to be strong. I want to have courage, I want not to be afraid, but…I don't know *how.* If you're there…if you exist…if you're not just a beautiful story…*help me.*"

The silence in the room was icy. Then suddenly into my mind came the phrase: "Take my yoke upon you, and learn of me; for I am meek and lowly in heart: and ye shall find rest unto your souls. For my yoke is easy and my burden is light."

I didn't know my Bible then and was not aware that these were Jesus' own words. But in the months ahead, I was to learn that the only way for me to know the power and the strength of God was indeed to take Jesus' yoke upon me and learn of him. As those words passed slowly in front of my eyes on the television screen that seemed to have taken root in my brain, I found myself repeating a psalm I had learned in school over thirty years before and had long since forgotten.

"God is our refuge and strength, a very present help in trouble. Therefore will we not fear, though the earth be removed, and though the mountains be carried into the midst of the sea; Though the waters thereof roar and be troubled, though the mountains shake with the swelling thereof."

My voice trailed at this point, seeking for the next verse. Not finding it I heard myself saying, "God is in the midst of her; she shall not be moved: God shall help her, and that right early."

Once again I faltered. Then, with tremendous force, I heard myself crying out: "The Lord of hosts is with us; the God of Jacob is our refuge."

I lay back on the bed and gazed up at the ceiling, unable to believe what had just happened. I had cried out and he had answered me. Not in actual human words. Not in a voice I could identify. But by these precious verses that he had brought out of the depths of my subconscious and placed in the forefront of my mind, to show me that he was real. That he was there. That above all, he wanted to help me, to give me strength, and "that right early." That he was waiting to share the yoke with me.

As if mesmerized, I slowly got off the bed and heard

the clock in the hall chime eleven. Christopher began to sing to himself, and like a robot, I went into the nursery and picked him up, holding his warm, plump body close to me as I struggled to grasp what had happened. Could I believe it? Was it true that God was real, that Jesus was alive and would be my friend if I asked him? For a moment I faltered, not knowing where to draw the line between my imagination and the power of God's might. Everything in me longed to believe, longed to abandon myself into his loving arms and yet…

The doorbell rang furiously and still clutching Christopher in my arms, I ran down the stairs.

There was an irate man standing outside, and as soon as I opened the door, he began to spit invectives. Unknown to me, one of our dogs had apparently slipped out when the children left and, following the trail of this man's bitch in heat, had apparently got into his house and caused havoc. The "havoc" boiled down to muddy paw marks on the shining parquet floors and a vase of flowers overturned by his happily wagging tail.

I realized that it was extremely tiresome from his point of view, yet it was an accident.… But he refused to listen to my apologies or to my offers of help to repair the damage and, having spent his venom to the full, turned tail, announcing over his shoulder that if the dog was seen on his land again, he'd shoot it!

He slammed the outside door loudly as he left and I

collapsed on the hall settle, my fragile peace shattered. I hadn't yet realized that even if we have Jesus and he has overcome sin, we are still left with human nature, and there's a lot of it around. Until we come to terms with this fact and realize that, in spite of everything, we are the victors because he has won the victory for us, we are not going to have that peace that he left with his disciples and that he promises to all those who believe.

But this was during the years of the "me" generation. The era of instant everything. And I wanted my peace, my courage, and my trust the minute I put my money in the slot. I had yet to learn that there is someone else who is determined to keep us from rejoicing in all these blessings, who is determined to make the money stick so that the slot machine doesn't work. If he can drive in a wedge the minute a new believer sees the light of Jesus begin to dawn in his life, his task is so much easier because he's won them back to his side of the fence. Back with the defeated.

And that rainy morning when I so nearly came face to face with my Lord and acknowledged him as my Savior, Satan got in first. But the good seed had been sown and had not fallen on barren ground, and Jesus is patient, so patient, and willing to wait.

thirteen

W hen Jacques came home that evening, I didn't tell him what I had done. He looked tired and drawn and had obviously had a very busy day. Dinner was over and the children all in bed when he finally walked into the house, and I didn't want to add to his worries or to have him suggest staying home for a few days to trail around after me...just in case. In spite of my temporary setback, I felt that for the moment I could cope—badly—but I was keeping my head above water. At least I had done so for that one day.

I won't say it was easy. But somehow I struggled through, sailing my little boat alone across those endless miles of choppy gray sea. Occasionally there was a beautiful sunset. Occasionally I felt that land was sighted. But mostly it was just a never-ending stretch of gray waves beating ceaselessly around my fragile back and threatening to overturn it.

At the beginning of February, Jacques casually asked me whether I hadn't got an appointment with Dr. Dufour coming up. It was then that I told him I didn't intend ever to have an appointment with him again, that I had been off my medication for over a week and had no intention of going back on it.

Jacques didn't say anything for the moment, then he slowly nodded his head.

"Why are you nodding like that?" I asked.

He smiled. "I've been praying that you would have the strength to do it," he replied quietly, "and I know that Jenny and Claire have too. But I didn't want to influence you in any way."

He looked at me intently. "It was a tremendous decision to make," he murmured. "Are you *sure* you are all right?"

"As right as I was when I was stuffed with pills," I snapped and immediately regretted my irritation. "Thank you for praying for me," I ended lamely.

Jacques rarely spoke about his prayer life or mentioned who he was praying for, and I was surprised and touched that he had told me. It encouraged me to hang on and grit my teeth in the face of all the odds. As I'd told him, I was no worse than when I was on medication, though I couldn't say I was a whole lot better, either. The word *abortion* haunted me. And the terrible guilt was always there whether I was drugged or not.

But I grudgingly admitted that perhaps, after all, there was something in prayer. I had already forgotten, or like

Stephen's unasked question, deliberately dismissed from my mind that wonderful experience Jesus had given me on that stormy Monday morning.

Yet that tiny seed, planted in an Essex village church, watered and tended by the love of my Christian friends, finally began to germinate and push its way through the damp soil of my heart, until a warm May afternoon when Jesus at last penetrated the thick, enveloping fog that, over the months, had gradually been turning into a soft mist, as his Word and the prayers of those who loved him were finally breaking through the hard shell that surrounded my heart.

As I abandoned the broken pieces of my life into his hands and asked for his love and his grace to be poured into my aching heart, he showed me that in the burden of guilt that lay behind my despair, the only true, lasting healing was to be found in him. That a God who has acted throughout history is a God who can and will act today if we will only let him open up a pathway through the enveloping gloom of guilt and anguish and fear that bar our way.

It had never been part of his plan that I should destroy that little life growing within me—that anyone should destroy a human fetus. But he gave us free will, knowing full well what we would do with it, and not then knowing Jesus personally, I had abused his trust and used my free will wrongly. But even so, once the hard shell around my heart had been melted in the recognition of his love, then he gave me the words "For with thee is the fountain of life: in thy light shall we see light."

I didn't realize the full significance of those words at the time. It was only many years later, when God gave me a vision of what "might have been," that I understood what he meant here for me, and I acknowledged that his is indeed the fountain of life...of all life, even a life we willfully destroy.

⟶

That summer I walked with my Savior and learned his ways. I confessed my failures and inadequacies to him and above all, the pain, guilt, and anguish I still felt over the loss of my baby, which had been slowly dragging me down into the pit where Satan intended me to go.

Jesus was very gentle and loving and, as he promised in his Word, he forgave me.

I truly thought I had accepted his forgiveness, been cleansed by his spilled blood, and had forgiven myself for the crime I had committed. But there was still a part of me that I had not handed over. I had kept as a little personal luxury my self-loathing for what I had done. This can be a luxury once we are born again and know that Jesus loves us and accepts us just as we are. It manifested itself in my refusal to believe I could really be forgiven for the crime I committed—a sin that had already been wiped off Jesus' slate—and refusing to forgive myself.

How much I still had to learn! When I entered our sunny little church that first Sunday morning after our vacation, I discovered what a short way I had really traveled along the road toward him.

We had left home for longer than usual that summer, and as we only arrived back a day or two before school started, I had not had time to contact anyone. But when we walked into church that first Sunday morning after our return, I was aware of a suppressed excitement in the air.

Claire and her children were sitting near the front, and as they didn't usually attend our church, I wondered a little why they were there. I didn't see Jenny or Lucille, but the church was unusually full so I imagined that they must be somewhere in the crowd. It was only at the end of the service, when the vicar announced that there was to be a double christening, that I had any inkling of what was happening.

From the back of the church, there was a flurry of people coming in from the porch. The little ones all came out of the Sunday school and walked solemnly to the font, and as the vicar approached it with the baptismal group, my heart suddenly stopped, then began beating wildly like a caged bird flapping its wings, crazy to escape.

Lucille was standing beside Jenny, who had a baby in her arms. Next to Jenny was a woman I didn't recognize but whom I gathered must be her younger sister because they looked so alike, also with a baby cradled lovingly to her. The three women were smiling dreamily, gazing down at the tiny bundles while David and Lionel and a cloud of family guests stood behind. I noticed Caroline, tall like her father, and the boys clustered around the font. Lucille's three were standing solemnly in the clutches of proud grandparents.

As the vicar took the baby from Jenny's sister's arms, the blood began to pound in my ears, and I held tightly onto the pew for support, my knuckles turning white with the effort. Jacques looked down at me anxiously and slipped his arm through mine, but I couldn't look at him. All I could see were those two bundles and Jenny and Lucille standing there, radiant in their motherhood.

If only I had been warned. If only I had known, it wouldn't have come as such a shock. But we had been away for almost two months, and the babies must have been born just after we left. In the excitement of the past few months and the continual go of the holidays, I had momentarily forgotten.

"Samuel David, I baptize thee," I heard the words through the pounding.

"Jennifer, I baptize thee…" the words came again.

A girl and a boy. I vaguely wondered which belonged to whom. I couldn't understand why Jenny and her sister should be holding the babies, then it struck me that, of course, Samuel must be Jenny's baby and her sister the godmother, and that Jenny was godmother to Lucille's baby, her namesake. How strange. Jenny, who had looked forward to a girl had a fourth boy, and Lucille, who had obviously hoped for a boy to balance up her family had a third daughter. I smiled wryly. Never get what you want in life, I thought. Then, seeing how happy they both were with the babies they had, I knew that, at the moment, if I could have been there with them, I wouldn't have minded *what* sex the child I was giving for baptism was, if only I could hold it and love it and watch it grow.

"Oh no," I whispered as I felt that familiar hot, stinging feeling rise behind my eyes. "Not now."

But there was no stopping them. The tears came trickling down my face. Glancing surreptitiously around, I saw that I was not alone. This moving double dedication had touched many in the congregation and countless cheeks were glistening with tears.

As we left the church, I avoided going over to Jenny and Lucille. It wasn't difficult; there was a crowd pressing all around them, admiring the babies. Caroline was standing on the porch as we went through.

"Not too disappointed?" I asked.

"Oh, no," she breathed, her eyes, which were so like her mother's, shining brightly. "He's *gorgeous*. Anyway, a sister wouldn't have been much use to me, really; she'd be so much younger. I'm very happy with my new little brother, and Roland is delighted. Aren't you, Roly-poly?" she inquired of her plump, six-year-old brother who was swinging from her hand.

"Ye-e-e-e-s," he chanted, pirouetting on the spot. "I'm going to teach him to play football."

"Not immediately, I hope," Jacques laughed, ruffling the little boy's hair as we passed.

We left the church without greeting either Jenny or Lucille, though I had a word with Lionel's mother, who detached herself from the crowd and came over to speak to us. Everybody seemed so thrilled with the new babies, and all fears and difficulties appeared to have been swept aside in the joy of their arrival.

I felt like a worm, not to be rejoicing with them.

fourteen

ou're going to have to face up to seeing the baby sooner or later," Jacques said quietly, not looking up from his paper as I walked back into the drawing room after putting down the phone. "Why do you keep procrastinating? That's the second time you've told Jenny you're not free when she's asked you over."

I bit my lip and sat down opposite him by the crackling fire.

October had arrived, bringing with it gloriously warm, golden days. But the evenings were chilly, and we were pleased to gather in front of the fire's comforting glow once dinner was over and peace finally descended on the house.

It was now almost two weeks since the christening, and I was still trying to pretend that it hadn't happened—as if I could go on for the rest of my life ignoring the fact that two of my closest friends now had an addition to their families. I had brought the matter before my Lord and asked him to help me but, although I didn't realize it then, I was the blockage. I was the one who was refusing to face up to the reality of the present situation. Refusing, in fact, to forgive myself although Jesus had made it abundantly clear, through his Word and his tenderness toward me, that he had forgiven me and placed my sin as far from me as the east is from the west. I had been washed by his precious blood and made as white as snow.

But deep down inside me, I think I didn't want to believe it. I didn't want to forget, I was afraid to forget, as a person fears to forget the face of a loved one who suddenly dies. I felt guilty at the thought that, with time, this searing experience could fade from my memory, and in order to keep it alive, I kept lashing myself and allowing that insidious magnet to draw me to the dreaded word. Seeing my two friends so obviously happy, my innate self-pity reared its ugly head and kept slyly telling me that their happiness could have been mine...if only...

I sighed and Jacques read my thoughts.

"More, 'if onlys'?" He smiled.

I picked up my tapestry angrily, irritated by his perception. Why did he always have to be right? He sensed my irritation and didn't pursue the matter further. But the remark had hit home and I wondered just where I had gone wrong. Why, since my return from vacation, I couldn't be "happy" like all my Christian friends. I was such a baby in Jesus then and hadn't realized that happiness is only part of the whole and basically comes when one stops looking for the "high" in our Christian walk and starts taking that radiance that we see when we first come to him into the business of daily living.

When I returned home that September, I had been full of enthusiasm for the school year that was about to start, determined to work for Jesus to the limit of my strength. But it was only as I began exhausting myself in this process without finding the great peace and fulfillment I sought that he gently showed me that it was not what I could do for him that mattered, but what he could do through me when I yielded totally to his will for my life. But it took time and I wasn't there yet.

Like most new Christians, I had begun on the right road. But as the first radiance inevitably wore off and everyday life began to crowd in on me and, at the same time, crowd out Jesus—the devil and his minions had certainly helped me in this instance—instead of remaining in the newness and freshness of his love, resting totally in him, I had started to do things in my own strength. To *work for him* instead of allowing him to *work through me*. And the result was beginning to show in my increasing busyness and resultant irritation.

"I'm tired," I announced, folding up the tapestry. "I think I'll go to bed."

"You do that," Jacques said, smiling at me over the top of his paper, "I won't be long."

And he bent to poke the remnants of the smoldering logs into one last blaze.

All next morning my husband's words of the previous evening rang in my ears. I couldn't stop thinking about what they had implied and wondered whether I was, in fact, dwelling morbidly on what "might have been," my "if onlys," as Jacques called them. Running away from something that, in the end, I should not be able to escape—in short, refusing to face up to reality.

Dropping Yves off at the school gate after lunch, I decided on an impulse to go see Jenny, break once and for all the fetter that, in its relentless grip of remorse, was binding me to the past. I knew she would most likely be at home; it was feeding time, and she wasn't the kind to worry about my turning up unannounced.

As I drew into her drive and slowed down before the front door, I noticed Lucille's car parked round by the side entrance and, in a panic, put my foot on the accelerator in an attempt to get away. But Jenny had seen me and flung open an upstairs window.

"What a lovely surprise!" she called, leaning out. "Come on in, Lucille's here. We've just had a scratch lunch after our monthly visit to the pediatrician, and I'm about to make some coffee."

I felt I couldn't face seeing both babies at once, but hadn't seen Lucille's car quickly enough to be able to make my escape.

As I walked into the hall, Jenny ran lightly down the stairs and hugged me warmly. She hadn't got her figure back yet and was still very round. Lucille came out of the dining room holding her baby in her arms.

"We've just finished lunch," she announced briskly, "but this one was too impatient to wait for hers."

I followed her into the children's playroom. Lucille hadn't changed a bit: looking at her tall, thin figure it was impossible to believe that she had so recently had her fourth baby. She plonked Jennifer on a shawl on the floor, and as she did so, Samuel began to cry lustily in his pram outside the open window.

"Oh, dear," I apologized. "Has my car awakened him?"

"No." Jenny laughed, going through into the garden and picking him up. "It's time, isn't it, my love?"

She held her baby close to her, and he looked at me curiously, blinking through sleep-filled eyes.

Samuel was not a pretty baby. He was bald and looked like a prizefighter, whereas his parents were a remarkably handsome couple. Jennifer, on the other hand, was beautiful. A little porcelain doll with tight black curls on her tiny head. I marveled that plain Lucille could have produced anything so exquisite.

"Here," said Jenny, handing me her little son. "Hold him a minute. I'll bring in the coffee and then I'll feed him. He'll behave himself as long as he's the center of attention."

And she disappeared into the kitchen, returning with the tray. Jennifer looked up at me from her position on the floor, studying my face intently: her deep blue eyes, the color of soft purple violets, reminded me of Christopher's when he was born.

"She's gorgeous," I murmured.

Lucille looked down at her daughter without emotion.

"Yes," she said practically, "she's not really much of a nuisance."

Jenny looked up as her son sucked contentedly.

"You know you're dotty about her," she teased.

But Lucille wasn't betraying anything.

"I think we all are," she answered. "Now what about this coffee? Do you want me to pour?"

As I sipped the warm brew, Jenny looked across at me.

"It *is* nice to see you," she said. "It seems such ages. You'd just left when Sam arrived, and Jacques was away on business so I wasn't able to let you know."

I nodded.

"When did he arrive?" I inquired for want of something better to say.

"When expected," said Lucille practically, "on the nineteenth. This little madam kept us all waiting till the twenty-fifth."

As she looked down at her daughter, who had now closed her eyes and was sleeping peacefully, I detected just a glimmer of emotion in her angular face.

"I'm sure she was worth the wait," I murmured.

Lucille nodded but didn't immediately reply. Then, to my astonishment, I saw tears shining in her eyes. Lucille, who never ever showed even a glimmer of emotion.

"To think," she whispered as they threatened to over-flow down her cheeks, "if I'd had my way, she would never have been born."

Both Jenny and I stared at her, speechless, unable to believe what we had just heard. Lucille seemed to have flung all her built-in reserve to the wind.

"I didn't want her," she said tightly. "She was a mistake I wanted to get rid of…and if I'd had the choice, I'd have had her aborted. My doctor wouldn't help, and I knew it was no good asking Lionel.…"

"Lucille," Jenny whispered, *"don't."*

"But it's *true,*" Lucille flashed. "I was desperate. We'd just sunk everything in Lionel's practice. He needed my help. The flat was far too small for us as it was, and I thought that her arrival when we were so short of money and space and had established our life was a disaster. I resented her. . .even hated her. . .until you rescued me."

She turned and smiled wanly at Jenny, the tears now glistening on her cheeks.

"*I* didn't rescue you," Jenny said softly, "Jesus did."

"Yes, but if it hadn't been for you, I might never have met him," Lucille replied.

"But you *did* meet him," Jenny answered.

"Only in the nick of time," Lucille choked. She covered her face with her hands as the tears ran through her fingers and fell onto her brown tweed skirt. "I don't know what it would have done to Lionel, or to our marriage, if I'd got rid of the baby," she sobbed.

"Don't torture yourself, Lucille," Jenny said gently.

Lucille looked up and, fishing in the pocket of her cardigan, pulled out a hankie and began scrubbing her face with it.

"Sometimes I think I need to be tortured," she replied briskly, "when I think of what could have happened. Thank God I *didn't* have the choice. I can't imagine life without her; she's such a joy to us all, and the other three absolutely adore her. They were all so close that none of them really knew what it was to have a baby in the house, and now they've got one, they're thrilled." She blew her nose loudly.

"As for Lionel…anyone would think he'd just become a father for the first time; he's so completely taken with her and looks ten years younger. Funny, isn't it, how I thought we'd never manage. Our finances were so tight last year at this time, yet now the practice is going forward by leaps and bounds, and Jennifer will have her first birthday in our new house."

I looked up in surprise, grateful for the change of subject.

I seemed to have run the whole gamut of emotions since Lucille's startling confession. Anger, pain, guilt, resentment, and the inevitable self-pity. Why had I had to make a choice, and she had not been given the chance to do so? My shattered feelings rocked about inside me and gradually subsided and fell in place again as I took refuge behind my coffee cup.

"You didn't know, did you?" Lucille explained, obviously relieved to be on safe ground again after the outburst that, I think, had surprised her more than anyone else. "We've bought a plot of land, and building should begin soon after Christmas."

"Where?" I inquired eagerly.

"Well, not so far out in the wilds as these Sinclairs here," Lucille replied briskly, her old astringent self once again. "We like the country but not that much. No, it's in between here and Paris."

"So you'll still be able to be on all your committees?" I teased.

She laughed, and the conversation lapsed as each mother gazed down at her baby.

"Samuel's an unusual name," I volunteered finally, breaking the silence. "Don't often hear it nowadays. What made you choose it?"

Their other children all had more "modern" names: Caroline, Patrick, Martin, and Roland.

Jenny looked up.

"We thought about it very carefully," she answered. "David and I both wanted a name that was meaningful. One that would make Sam understand that he was really wanted. After all, coming as he has done so long after the others, he could wonder when he got older whether he was merely an afterthought.

I nodded. I did not see the implication but was relieved she had not used the word *mistake*.

"When we came to Samuel, we realized we had found the right name," Jenny continued. "You remember the story of Hannah in the Bible?"

I shook my head. Samuel rang a bell, but not Hannah.

"She was barren," Jenny explained, "and she promised God that if he would give her a son, she would give him back into his service."

She paused and looked down at her sleeping Samuel.

"He heard her prayer, and she kept her promise," Jenny went on softly. "Her son Samuel was one of the greatest prophets in the Old Testament."

She looked across at me and smiled.

"Samuel means 'asked of God,'" she said. "Knowing that, our Samuel couldn't possibly have any doubts about how much we all wanted him."

She bent down and kissed his shiny bald head.

"I don't suppose you're puzzling over why ours is called Jennifer," smiled Lucille.

"Well, no," I replied. "It's obvious."

"If she grows up to be like her namesake," Lucille went on, "we'll have nothing to complain about. She'll be a beautiful person…both inside and out."

Jenny looked up and smiled, taking the compliment

graciously and naturally, not making false protestations as I, and probably most women, would have done.

It was unusual for Lucille to be so flowery. It struck me that she hadn't added, "as long as she doesn't look like me," which I distinctly remember her saying when I had admired both Elizabeth and Beatrice as babies. And I realized that having become a committed Christian, having accepted Jesus as her personal Savior, had indeed made a difference in Lucille's life and in her attitude toward herself.

That complex about her plainness that had been apparent in the aside remarks she had often made, had completely disappeared. She had the assurance that Jesus loved her and accepted her, that he wanted her, in fact, just as she was. That it was he who had made her, and in his image: she was a child of God and beautiful in his eyes. Sitting there in the peaceful silence, I realized that I had not yet accepted myself as I was, as God had made me. Words from the Bible came floating into my mind: "Love your neighbor as yourself." And I understood that I hadn't learned to love myself, and if I didn't love myself, how could I possibly love my neighbor? I wouldn't know how to begin. For loving someone completely, as Jesus means us to love, means loving unconditionally, that agape love that our Savior showers on us all. And in that unconditional, agape love is forgiveness.

"Are you going to the retreat next Friday?" Jenny broke in on my musing.

"What retreat?" I asked.

"Oh, rather like the one Claire took you to last winter," she went on. "Hasn't she called you? She intended to."

"Perhaps she has," I answered, "and I've been out."

"Call her when you get back," Jenny urged. "She's always at home when the children arrive from school. We can't go, rather out of things for the moment, but I'm sure you'd enjoy it. Claire had heard the speaker before and says she's very inspiring."

"I'll see," I replied absently.

But I didn't have to call Claire.

By the time I got back, she had already called me, and was in fact just leaving a message with one of the boys as I entered the house. I took the receiver, knowing exactly why she had called, and was already mentally reorganizing my week so as to be free on Friday.

As I put down the phone, I had a strange feeling inside me. I couldn't define it, but I realized that Jacques had been right. I had been living on "if onlys" despite my new walk with Jesus. Somehow the afternoon had been cathartic and therapeutic. I had faced up to reality, seen both babies, even held them, and not collapsed in a flood of tears. And that insight into Lucille's new attitude had shown me flaws in my own Christian walk and somehow put me on the road to recovery.

My heart began to sing freely, like a bird in a tree waking up to the fact that it is spring and everything is fresh and new and clothed in green. I didn't know what I expected from this retreat or what I thought the speaker could do to touch that hidden depth in me that needed cleansing.

I do know that what I received from her was certainly not what I expected.

fifteen

Claire was a very organized person, and her punctuality was legendary. So when, as the hall clock struck nine, I did not hear her light step on the path outside the front door, I was surprised. But when it struck the quarter hour and she still hadn't appeared, I began to wonder whether I had not mistaken the day.

Crossing to the telephone table, I looked down at the diary. No, the day was right and the time was nine. But it was now nine-twenty. I picked up the receiver and dialed Claire's number. As it began to ring, I heard a car pull up, followed by the sound of running footsteps and saw Claire through the hall window. Picking up my bag I went quickly to meet her. She was breathless and not her usual impeccable self—certainly not living up to her reputation of never having a hair out of place.

"I'm *so* sorry," she breathed as we ran together to her car. "We might just make the beginning if we're lucky with the lights and the traffic…but we'll need a miracle."

She smiled wanly at me as she started the engine.

"I'm afraid we've had a dreadful night," she confessed. "Quentin and I didn't get to bed till after five and we slept right through the alarm. Usually when I'm going out for the day I get up early and leave everything prepared. But it was only when Catherine walked into our bedroom at seven-thirty to find out what had happened that I realized we'd overslept, and it's been a mad rush ever since."

Claire's husband was an ordained minister who, I presumed, must occasionally have disturbed nights. But it had never occurred to me that his night calls could include her. I raised my eyebrows inquiringly, not wanting to ask a direct question in case it was something she wasn't able to talk about.

"You probably don't remember the Goddards," she inquired. "They were at that barbecue at Jenny's where we met."

I frowned trying to think back.

"An older couple," she went on, "well not so much older; Liliane's just fifty, Maurice is about fifty-five."

I shook my head; neither the name nor the description rang a bell.

"Maurice rang us at about midnight in a dreadful state—their daughter had committed suicide."

"Oh *no*," I gasped, "how terrible."

"It *is*," Claire sighed. "We both went round immediately and stayed till their son arrived. He lives near Bordeaux and drove through the night to get here."

"But *why?*" I asked.

Claire paused and bit her lip.

"Oh, I may as well tell you," she said at last. "It's not giving away any secrets. The police found the note in her coat pocket so it'll all come out at the inquest. I can't believe the local papers will miss making it headlines. Maurice is on the town council so it will be a great scoop for them. Anyway, I feel I need to talk about it. Quentin and I are both reeling under the shock."

She paused again and felt for her hankie. I handed her mine, and she blew her nose loudly before continuing.

"She was to have been married at Christmas," she choked. "Only twenty-three. Then, out of the blue, she does that."

For a moment Claire was unable to speak and I waited, a terrible sadness engulfing me.

"Claire," I said gently. "We don't *have* to go to this retreat. If you'd rather turn around and go home or come back home with me, I don't mind in the least."

"No, it's all right," Claire said, wiping her eyes, "we'll go. I need to get away from the world more than ever today. It's just that…they're such dear friends of ours, and I can't bear it for them. They've got to live the rest of their lives with this terrible tragedy hanging over them. Luckily Eric, their son, is married and they have two delightful grandchildren who will be a comfort to them but…all the same."

Her voice threatened to break again.

"If *only* Valerie had come to talk to Quentin, I'm sure it could have been sorted out," Claire went on. "But we didn't know anything about it. Her parents didn't either. It's been a terrible shock to everyone. Apparently when she was a student away from home, she became pregnant by the man she was going to marry at Christmas, as it happens. But he had finished his studies and just left to do military service in Algeria. It was at the time of the troubles out there. She couldn't get hold of him and she panicked."

As Claire paused, something began to dawn in my mind and I knew exactly what Valerie had done. The magnet was drawing me yet again toward the word that refused to stop haunting me.

"She had an abortion," Claire said, quietly gazing straight ahead through the car window so that I should not see the tears threatening to spill over and tumble down her cheeks again.

"She never told her fiancé about it but, as always happens, when he came home, someone else did. They had a terrible row and the engagement was broken. There again, if only she'd confided in someone. Her parents didn't know why they'd parted; she refused to discuss it. Then about a year ago, they came together again and everything seemed wonderful. All the arrangements had been made for the wedding, they'd even gotten an apartment. Her fiancé was to have moved in on November 1. Then yesterday evening

Valerie rang Liliane saying she wouldn't be home for dinner, as she and Guy were going to measure the apartment for wallpaper and not to worry if she was late. At ten o'clock a man walking his dog in the forest found her hanging from a tree. He wasn't young and is now in the hospital suffering from shock."

Her voice broke again.

"There was a note in her pocket for her parents telling them the whole story. She said she couldn't live with the guilt and remorse and felt her life with Guy would be shadowed by it. Even though he had forgiven her, she couldn't forgive herself."

Claire's voice had fallen to a whisper, and the tears were now flowing freely down her cheeks and down mine too. Neither of us made any attempt to stop them. How well I understood this poor girl's feelings, being unable to forgive herself for what she had done. I had been living with the same guilt for almost a year now, and I knew only too well what she had gone through. But I had Jacques and the children. For me, there was no turning back, whereas she was on the threshold of a new life, and she had been afraid to take the plunge into happiness in case that happiness might one day be sullied and broken by the past insidiously invading it.

"Her poor parents," I whispered at last.

"It's terrible for them," Claire gulped. "And what is so stupid is that they are such precious, loving people. They would have understood if only she'd confided in them. Oh, if only we could say something to help them…but what can anyone say?"

"Nothing," I replied blankly. "Absolutely nothing. Just be there and show them you love them, that's all."

I knew from my own experience just how much a caring presence and unconditional love meant at times.

"Yes," she sighed, "we can do that, I suppose. But, oh, how one longs to do so much more."

"There's nothing more you can do," I reassured her.

Claire shook her head sadly.

"You'd be surprised," she said quietly, "how many women are on tranquilizers because of abortions."

I looked up at her inquiringly, not surprised at all.

"Many women come to Quentin for help. Not necessarily members of his church. Many of them not even churchgoers. He says he hasn't met one yet who doesn't afterward feel terrible guilt about an abortion. And a lot of doctors he's talked to have said the same thing. It doesn't always happen immediately, but it comes out sooner or later. Quentin feels so helpless because there's nothing he can do once it's happened. He can only point them to Jesus and his forgiveness, and they're not all prepared to accept him. It's heartbreaking."

I nodded absently, memories tumbling crazily in my tangled mind as we lapsed into silence. And I longed to tell Claire that I knew what she was talking about. That I knew how Valerie must have felt because I had gone through it. And that her husband was so right in what he said. Guilt always tracks us down sooner or later.

But, as on that cold Sunday afternoon eight months earlier, no words came. I was still unable to forgive myself, and in spite of all I had experienced to the contrary, all the acceptance and unconditional love I had received, I was still afraid of condemnation. Perhaps this is one of the lesser pains, other than the dreadful guilt of an abortion, the terrible fear of not being accepted because of what one has done. I understood the fear that had driven Valerie to take her life.

We arrived at the retreat just in time.

We'd missed the welcoming coffee and the chorus singing that preceded the speaker, but I don't think either of us felt very much like singing that morning, nor like joining in with the friendly chatter of participants sipping coffee as they waited for the meeting to begin.

The theme of the talk was forgiveness.

As Claire and I settled into our seats, trying to put the previous night's tragedy out of our minds for a few hours and concentrate on what the speaker had to say, I marveled at the way God programs and organizes our lives. Had I not suddenly decided to go to Jenny's that afternoon the week before and heard Lucille's devastating confession and seen the subtle change in her, I might never have realized that forgiveness is what I needed to know about. It was something I had only touched superficially and paid lip service to and which was sadly lacking in my attitude toward myself and toward Jesus.

The speaker was not unlike the one who had "not impressed" me earlier in the year when I was still groping in the dark. But this time, the ground of my heart was raked and ready. When she opened up her own life and experience, her words seemed to speak straight to me, enabling me to lay my heart bare and find healing.

As we left the conference hall after the afternoon session and walked toward the dining room for tea, I knew that I needed to talk to her. I had attempted to do so after lunch, but there had been so many women around her that I had hung back, my pride not wanting to admit to the world at large that I, too, needed help and guidance. But now I knew that this was my last opportunity. In a few minutes Claire and I would be speeding through the late afternoon traffic on our way home. I might never see this woman again, and something told me that she could give me some words I needed to hear.

Had I known then what those words would be, I wonder whether I would have waited for her so expectantly.

I watched her chatting with the organizer of the retreat, and my heart began to beat in a panic-stricken fashion, afraid that someone would claim her attention, that Claire and I would have to leave, and the opportunity lost forever. But at that moment, the organizer was called to the telephone. I saw her excuse herself and walk away, leaving the speaker alone for the first time since she arrived. Quickly putting down my cup, I hurried over to where she was standing sipping her tea.

She looked up and smiled as I appeared in front of her.

"I'd like to have a word with you...if you have the time," I faltered.

I hadn't the faintest idea what I was going to say. But I knew that I had to talk to her.

"Of course," she said gently, putting down her cup and drawing me into an alcove made by the long window.

She was a tall, good-looking woman, very simply dressed in a tailored gray flannel suit, the tie of her cream blouse loosely knotted at her throat. Her soft white hair was drawn back into a small bun at the nape of her neck. I knew from what she had said that she was a widow and that her children were grown up and married. She had told us that her husband had been head of a theological college and had died an agonizing death from cancer some years before. She had also told us that in her anguish she had questioned why, after a life of unswerving devotion to his Lord, God would allow him to suffer so terribly, and her husband had quietly replied, "I chose my master, but I didn't choose my road."

Those words had had a profound effect upon me. In spite of everything, I was still at the stage when I imagined that becoming a Christian was a kind of insurance policy against all ills. But this woman had taught me the contrary.

She had been so open with us about her own feelings, her fears, and her angers, which she had given over to Jesus. She had suffered deeply, and yet she had that transparent radiance that comes from being honed in God's fire. I identified with her when she confessed her feelings of self-pity and even of anger when her only daughter married an Australian and went with him to the other end of the world. She was so warm. So human. She didn't pretend to be a superwoman who never felt any doubt or pain just because she was a Christian. She admitted her feelings, but she also shared her secret that confessing her weaknesses and receiving Jesus' forgiveness had made all the difference in her life.

We sat down side by side on the red velvet window seat, and she patiently waited for me to begin.

Stumbling over my words, I haltingly told her the story of my abortion and the fact that, although I had become a Christian and asked forgiveness, deep down I couldn't believe that Jesus could forgive me for committing such a crime. And I couldn't forgive myself either.

I paused and took a deep breath, trying to find the right words.

"This attitude is poisoning my faith, my whole attitude to my new life in him, and destroying any Christian witness I could hope to give," I finally blurted out.

Her hazel eyes looked at me penetratingly for a few

seconds, while I sat there confidently waiting for the words of comfort I expected to hear. And then they came.

"What makes you think you're so special?" she said abruptly.

I gasped, completely taken aback.

"I…don't," I stammered.

"Yes, you do," she replied, and her voice seemed hard. There was an uncomfortable silence in which we each waited for the other to say something. I half rose. This wasn't at all what I had come to hear. But she put her hand on my arm, and I fell back upon the window seat.

"If you say you believe that Jesus died for our sins…and you do believe it?"

I nodded, not daring to raise my eyes.

"Then you're making a mockery of his death."

I could hardly believe my ears.

"He died that agonizing death on the cross for the sins of the whole world. So that we should be made clean, purified. The worst sinner can receive forgiveness, no matter how heinous the crime. That murderer who was crucified with him was pardoned and assured that he would be with Jesus in Paradise that very same day."

She paused before shooting her next arrow.

"But that's not good enough for you. You think you are so important you must have some kind of special dispensation…. Jesus' death wasn't enough to cleanse you from sin. You can't be lumped with everyone else and receive his cleansing as they have done. No, you have to have VIP treatment."

She looked at me intently, forcing my eyes upward to meet hers.

"Do you want to crucify him again?" she said tightly. "Is that what you need in order to be forgiven? Is one crucifixion not enough for you?"

She took a deep breath.

"Beware of the pious fraud in you that says, 'I have no misgivings about Jesus…only about myself.' None of us ever had misgivings about ourselves. But we *do* have misgivings about Jesus. You're annoyed because he can forgive and you can't."

She stopped and looked me straight in the eye.

"If Jesus said that if we confess our sins he is faithful and just to forgive us our sins and to cleanse us from all unrighteousness," she enunciated, stressing each word clearly, "then he meant what he said. He didn't add that the promise held good for everyone but Noreen Riols. That she, being made out of a superior mold, would need a special dispensation."

I was mortified and speechless as we sat together in silence. Then she gently took my hand and I looked up into her eyes, which were now full of compassion. I think they must have held the same expression as was in Jesus' eyes the night before his crucifixion when the cock crowed the second time and he looked across the courtyard to Peter, the disciple who had sworn that he would die for him and yet had so quickly deserted him when the hour of testing came.

"I'm sorry, my dear," she said kindly. "It was the only way. But you're not alone. Many fall into Satan's trap of being unable to believe they're forgiven, and no amount of reasoning will get them out of it. Only shock treatment will. You *must* believe that Jesus wants us to turn our backs on our mistakes and, instead of being perpetually submerged and defeated by them, to hand them over to him so that out of evil he is able to bring good. Doesn't the Bible say: 'All things work together for good to them that love God'? And when he says *all* things, he means *all things.*"

She released my hand.

"You *are* forgiven," she went on softly. "Now believe it and forgive yourself. You cannot undo the past, but you can resolve to love and serve him with all your heart in the future…from this very minute, in fact."

She paused and this time took both my hands in hers.

"Let's ask him to send his healing spirit into your heart and life," she said softly, "and close this dreadful wound." As she began to pray, tears began to flow again. But they were healing tears. Cleansing and renewing my heart, which had so firmly refused, up to that moment, to abandon all to God. I sincerely believed I had done so. But I had been sincerely wrong. The surrender hadn't been complete. As long as there was one small area, one tiny bridgehead where Satan could gain a foothold, one tiny corner of my life that was not totally yielded to Jesus, I had been in danger. The devil *had* gained a foothold, taken a last-ditch stand and fought fiercely to the very end. And had almost won.

Now I knew that I was whole and victorious. Jesus had won the victory for me many centuries ago, and Satan was a defeated enemy.

I also knew that even in situations of our own making, Jesus can rechannel our mistakes and abject failures onto a path where his name will be glorified.

As I rose from the velvet seat, a last ray of afternoon sunshine came slanting in through the window, falling onto her serene face. And I knew that coming to her had not been a mistake. The steely words she had darted into my heart had been necessary. And I vowed that, from that moment onward, I would look firmly and with hope toward the future…with no looking back.

"Ask Jesus to give you courage every morning." She smiled as we parted. "Don't make wild promises about never falling again. We're only human, and they're impossible to keep. Just ask for courage for twenty-four hours and you'll be surprised at how the day unfolds. The Lord gives us our ticket as we step on the train, not on the way to the station. And he will give you courage and hope and joy in daily doses if you sincerely seek him and ask him for it."

And I knew that she was right.

As Claire and I walked back to the car, back to the world, my heart ached for Valerie, who had had no one to tell her that she was forgiven. Who had preferred to take her life rather than live with her guilt. And for her parents who would carry this tragedy and the unanswered questions, perhaps even the conviction that they had failed her, with them to the grave. The story of Jesus and the woman caught in adultery, about to be stoned by the hypocritical religious leaders of the day, came to my mind. His words: "neither do I condemn you" rang in my ears. Had Valerie only known that he didn't condemn her, she could perhaps have forgiven herself and obeyed his parting words to the woman: "Go in peace and sin no more."

"Lord Jesus," I cried out in my heart. "Help me to show others what your love can do. That in you there is healing for every wound. In you is no condemnation."

I didn't know how he could use me, or even if he would use me, but I was offering myself as his channel to spread this wonderful, blessed unconditional love.

Yet I knew that I couldn't do it by myself.

sixteen

That cold, astringent shower, that icy hailstorm of healing words administered to me on a golden October afternoon just five months after my conversion was to mark the end of my "babyhood," my bottle-fed existence as a Christian, and it brought me into a new relationship, a new spiritual dimension, as I realized that my life was not going to consist of jumping, like a hind, from mountaintop to mountaintop. I learned that, in fact, my mountaintop experiences were going to be, in the future, the exception, rather than the rule. I had now to face life as a child of God, preparing to be the adult he wanted me to be.

It was not long afterward that he showed me, in a dream, a dream that was so vivid it was almost a vision, what he had wanted me to be.

I was in a room, a large oblong room paneled in dark wood. It had smooth, shining parquet floors and looked like the ballroom of a stately home. But strangely enough it was empty except for one beautiful portrait hanging on the wall at the far end. The picture had a light about it, and as I walked toward it, I was struck by the serenity of the woman portrayed. She wasn't beautiful in the classical sense, but she had something that drew my attention, that immediately attracted me to her. As I gazed up at the portrait, alone in that quiet room, Jesus appeared beside it and stood looking down at me.

"What kind of person do you think she is?" he said, pointing to the portrait.

I gazed intently at those tranquil features.

"She's not beautiful," I answered reflectively, "but she has something about her."

He smiled.

"What, exactly?"

"I don't know," I pondered. "A serenity…a goodness perhaps."

"Compassion?"

"Oh, yes," I breathed. "Certainly compassion. She looks as if she's a lovely person…both inside and out," I added, remembering Lucille's words about Jenny.

"Would you have liked to have her for a friend?"

"Who wouldn't?" I laughed. "She seems so warm and kind."

He paused and looked at me intently.

"If you were in trouble, do you think you could call on her? Would you *want* to?"

I was becoming more and more intrigued and looked up at him inquiringly. But he merely smiled enigmatically.

"Yes," I replied thoughtfully, "I'm sure I could. She seems to have all the qualities expected of a Christian."

He nodded.

"But why are you asking me all these questions?" I pursued. "Who is she?"

He didn't reply immediately. Then, reaching up, he carefully took the portrait down from the wall and turned it around, holding it up for me to see. On the other side was the reflection of my own face.

"I don't understand," I whispered. "What do you mean?"

Jesus carefully hung the picture back on the wall, the right side facing us before replying, and the woman looked down on us once again.

"Who is she?" I asked hoarsely.

Turning to face me, he said quietly, "She's the woman I'd planned for you to be."

And this time he wasn't smiling. There was an immense sadness in his eyes.

"Lord," I cried brokenly, and as I burst into tears, the dream faded. But the sadness in my Savior's eyes remained with me, shatteringly present as I realized how I had failed him. Jesus had had that plan for my life since the beginning of time. Yet my wallowing had almost obliterated him and put self-pity on the throne as I gradually turned into a craving spiritual sponge. In my stubbornness I had turned my back on his perfect plan and gone my own way.

Humbly kneeling in prayer that morning, I thanked him for what he had shown me and asked him to forgive me for failing him. As his wonderful peace and love flowed through me, I knew that although in the past I had wandered very far from his path, in his perfect plan, it is never too late to return and with his help pick up the pieces and start again on the right road.

Out of these experiences, I entered into a new and deeper relationship with Jesus. I learned that the meaning of prayer is basically to get to know God, to reach out and touch him, not to receive instant answers. That God's purpose is not just to answer our prayers, but that through our prayers, this closest of all relationships, we could come to know his mind and to pray, as Jesus did, in our Father's will.

Up until that moment, I had thought I knew what prayer was, that I had sounded its depths. But Jesus revealed to me that the prayer he tells us about in the Gospels, that prayer that really reaches out and touches the Father, stems from repentance, and that out of repentance, that deep, heart-searching repentance I felt after this experience, a repentance that does not bring with it a sense of sin, but rather an overwhelming sense of absolute unworthiness and utter helplessness, comes cleansing.

Jesus' words—"I am the vine, ye are the branches: He that abideth in me, and I in him, the same bringeth forth much fruit: for without me ye can do nothing"—pierced through my mask and showed me myself as I really was, as he saw me. I finally surrendered all in total obedience to him, the kind of obedience that involves not only the emotions but penetrates every fiber of the believer's mind, body, and spirit, and is the key that opens the door to freedom— the freedom that only absolute trust in a loving Savior can bring.

Entering into this new dimension, this deeper prayer life, I discovered that this kind of obedience actually changes us and totally changes our relationship with our Creator. It was as if the words in 1 Corinthians 13, "for now we see through a glass darkly," came true. Until then I had been peering through a glass darkly, but now, suddenly, I saw him face-to-face. And when that happened, I was at last able to put the painful memory of my abortion behind me and accept that what had been done could not be undone and that he could make all things new. As the Bible promises, "the old had gone, the new had come."

I even managed to rise above my emotions when, a few years later, Christopher came home from school one morning and announced that his friend's baby sister had arrived during the night.

"Why do I have to be the littlest?" he demanded belligerently. "You gave Yves me, and all the others had a baby. Why can't I have a baby sister too?"

I tried to explain to him that a family had to stop somewhere, but he was feeling fractious and wouldn't let the matter drop.

"It's not fair," he grumbled. "*I'd* like to have a baby sister. It's no fun being the youngest."

That's probably it, I consoled myself as he went back to school, his football tucked under his arm, his grievance forgotten. It wasn't the baby sister he really wanted but not to be the youngest—to have someone to boss instead of being the one who was bossed by everyone else. Yet, at the back of my mind, there was a niggle of guilt. I knew he could have had a baby sister or brother. He wasn't meant to be the "littlest." And that small niggle wasn't suppressed quite as easily as I had expected it to be.

Sitting reading my Bible one morning a few days later, these words from the book of Proverbs sprang out at me: "There is a way which seemeth right unto a man, but the end thereof are the ways of death" (Proverbs 14:12).

I saw what the Lord was trying to point out to me. That his ways are not our ways and that what had seemed "right to man" at the time of my abortion was in the end "the ways of death."

God said in the Old Testament, "'I have set before you life and death, blessing and cursing: therefore choose life, that both thou and thy seed may live'" (Deuteronomy 30:19).

My heart went out to the many women who, perhaps

unwittingly, were at that very moment choosing wrongly, choosing the ways of death, only subsequently to suffer guilt and depression, fear and anxiety.

We can only speak authoritatively and honestly about the thing we know, out of the depth of our personal experience. I recall a conversation I had recently with a friend who had an abortion many years ago. She is not a committed Christian, and I asked her how she felt about it now, wondering if, after the lapse of time, her experience had been, emotionally, the same as mine.

"Looking back," she said reflectively, "I think that the abortion blighted my life."

She paused and gazed into the distance.

"I read recently," she continued quietly, "that one in seven married couples in Britain nowadays are unable to have children, many of them because of an early abortion, and it made me wonder whether my abortion wasn't the cause of the ectopic pregnancy I had ten years later. There doesn't seem to be any other explanation as to why I've never been able to have a baby."

Helen is an intelligent, extroverted, happily married woman in her midfifties: a woman who appears, on the outside to have everything, and yet...

"Luckily we were able to adopt, and our two boys have given us tremendous joy."

She smiled across at me.

"All things considered, I've had a very happy life, but

my one deep, lasting sorrow is that I've never had the supreme joy of holding my own baby in my arms and hearing its first cry."

Helen once again paused and gazed into that distance I was unable to penetrate.

"But I saw my baby," she ended softly. "Or what *would* have been my baby."

I looked up in surprise, not fully understanding.

"I was only seventeen when I became pregnant," she went on. "And in the late forties, nicely brought up girls didn't have illegitimate babies."

I nodded, remembering the terrible stigma placed on unmarried mothers in the pre- and immediate postwar years.

"I had the abortion at home," she continued. "The doctor gave me an injection to induce contractions and make the fetus come away, and he and my mother stayed with me until it happened. I was conscious all the time and saw it when it did come away."

Her lips tightened, and I could see that even after all these years, the memories were still alive and painful.

"It wasn't a mass of fetal jelly as the papers make us believe," she whispered. "It was a minute living human being...my baby."

In the ensuing silence, I think we two middle-aged women were both plunged back into "what might have been."

"I've never forgotten it," she said, looking up. "It may seem stupid, but each year, I still remember the day the baby would have been born. That's what I mean when I say it blighted my life…or certainly cast a shadow over it."

She sighed deeply.

"My baby's death was a death I wasn't allowed to mourn," she ended.

I understood only too well what she meant.

Since I had the abortion, I have come to the conclusion that this relatively simple operation goes much deeper than most people realize. Perhaps even deeper than the medical profession itself realizes, though I believe that counseling services are at last beginning to understand that it is not a "minor operation" that can be dismissed after a weekend's rest. The consequences and the ramifications burrow into areas way beyond the merely physical sphere and can cause long-lasting and devastating havoc in the psychological makeup of a woman, and sometimes even the mental health of the man who fathered the aborted child. It doesn't always happen immediately. But I doubt whether any woman, in the long run, actually escapes scot-free. Removing a fetus from the womb is not like removing an appendix, which is merely a physical amputation. With an abortion, the emotions are so intricately involved that they invariably end up being injured or even crushed.

I can't help thinking that if when a woman goes to her doctor requesting an abortion, he would just take the time and trouble to explain to her what that little life growing inside her looked like and what it was doing at that moment, she might, perhaps, change her mind.

Before performing a mastectomy, the surgeon is careful to warn a woman of the emotional trauma that follows in about 60 percent of all cases. The removal of a breast invariably gives rise to depression and the sense of something vital missing. And this is an operation where, basically, the woman does not have a choice.

But how much more should the removal of a growing baby from her body give rise to feelings of depression and emptiness, and an even deeper sense of loss? Especially when it need not have happened—the final decision being hers.

I don't believe we can act callously with unborn human life without ending by adopting the same attitude toward other human beings who might present a threat or be a nuisance to us. The elderly, the handicapped, people who are supposedly no longer useful or productive, or who are imperfect specimens. We forget that they are only useless or imperfect in our eyes…not in the eyes of God.

Legalized abortion is merely the thin edge of the wedge—a wedge that could force open endless possibilities for all age groups and all strata of society—possibilities that are not only endless but terrifying.

Since that cold January morning at Victoria Station

when the magnet began to draw me, inexorably, toward anything remotely connected with abortion, I have read much of which, in spite of my nursing training, I was ignorant.

I did not realize that even at four weeks a fetus not only has all its outer and inner organs but has brain waves, the criteria that determines whether a person is alive or not, that can be registered. At seven weeks it has a face with eyes, nose, lips, and tongue. It is, in fact, a tiny human being who can suffer.

My baby was almost twelve weeks old with every organ in place, a miniature of what it would have been at birth six months later. Even its minute, completely formed fingerprints would not have changed, except for size. All that remained for it to do was grow.

When I agreed to the abortion, I had no idea how the fetus was extracted from the womb. How many people do? But now that I do know, I am horrified. I wonder how many women who submit to an abortion, for whatever reason, know, as Helen discovered when it was too late, that the tiny creature is not a mass of fetal jelly but a live baby—their baby, whose heart rate increases as it shrinks from the abortionist's instrument as it is literally torn limb from limb. Finally having its skull crushed before being vacuumed out, like the dirt from under a carpet, and thrown into the bin.

Even our domestic pets are wrapped up and buried

when they die, and sadistic murderers who torture victims before committing cold-blooded, heinous crimes are humanely executed.

But that growing baby was innocent. It had committed no crime. Except that of being conceived.

I agonized over how we were ever going to teach the coming generation about the sanctity of human life. They would grow up to believe that unborn babies were things you either kept or threw away, according to adult whim. For them this slaughter would not only be normal but legal, something that was sanctioned and subsidized by the government.

And my heart bled for my grandchildren.

I have talked with women who say they have the right to do as they wish with their bodies. Maybe they sincerely believe they have. If we are Christians, we don't think that way because we know that our bodies do not really belong to us but are the temple, the home, in fact, of the Holy Spirit. And we do not have the right to defile it.

But if they are honest with themselves, I wonder if these emancipated women really believe that they have the right to condemn to death another human being who is under their protection, for whose life they are responsible and who is defenseless, sheltering in their body. Has no one explained to them that by agreeing to an abortion, it is not *their* bodies they are "doing as they like with"?

Disposing of? But the body of a child who in a few short weeks will be an independent human being? Doesn't that little baby share the same human rights as they do?

I hope it is ignorance of the procedure, wrong advice, or social pressures and not callousness that prompts the millions of abortions that are carried out every year. These are mostly social abortions, since those performed because of danger to the mother's life, fear of deformity to the child, or rape account for only 2 percent.

As these thoughts went around in my head, and the full horror of what I had done and what many women were, at that very moment, contemplating doing or had already done, I fell to my knees once again in an agony of hopelessness. Hopelessness because, once done, it was irrevocable.

As I knelt there, something inside me said, "Ask forgiveness of the baby to whom you denied life. Ask Jesus to show you that the child is with him."

It seemed such a preposterous idea that I sat back on my heels, momentarily stunned by the mere suggestion. Yet, as I thought about it, I realized that I had, after all, denied my child life. What was more natural than to ask its forgiveness?

I buried my face in my hands and asked Jesus to let me see my child so that I should know that it was with him. Gradually there rose before me that same picture of Jesus that I had seen in my dream, only this time he was in a meadow. It must have been spring because the grass covering his feet was fresh and green, and there were cowslips and little clusters of daisies dotted around. Behind him was a tall mauve mountain and a white cloud floated above it in a clear blue sky.

As I watched he held out his hand, and a barefooted little girl skipped happily toward him and looked up, smiling, into his face. She was wearing a deep blue dress, and her silver blond hair hung to her shoulders, curling softly at the ends. Jesus smiled down at her and motioned with his head for her to turn around, and as she did so, I gasped. Her face was that of Yves, her wide china-blue eyes, his eyes. The fine, silver-blond, softly curling hair, his hair as it had been when he was a little boy.

We looked at each other without moving, then, almost inaudibly, I whispered brokenly, "Forgive me." She gave me the loveliest smile and, looking up into Jesus' face, put her hand in his.

I remained kneeling for a long time, my face buried in my hands with the vision of my child in my mind, and I remembered God's words spoken through the prophet Joel: "I will pour out my spirit upon all flesh; and your sons and your daughters shall prophesy, your old men shall dream dreams, your young men shall see visions." I was unable to move as waves of gratitude washed through me. Gratitude not only for the precious vision that had just been given me, but gratitude for the things that had happened to me throughout my life. For the way I had been shown such unconditional love and understanding when I had expected judgment and condemnation.

As I knelt there, all those faces from the past—Judy, Adrian, Mary, Stephen, Simon Wing, Professor Ponting, Sister B.—rose before me and merged with the faces of my parents and Jacques in a smiling photograph as if they were saying, with Jesus, "neither do I condemn you." And I realized how God had put together the jigsaw of my life and made the pieces fit in spite of my early indifference. How, because I had finally turned to him, he in his mercy had made all things work for good.

And I think it was then that I understood that faith is not common sense. It defies common sense. Nor is it a pathetic sentiment. Faith is total confidence built on the eternal truth that God is love. We cannot see him with our mortal eyes. We don't always understand what he is doing. But we know *him*, the living God. And although faith does not always know where it is being led, it does know and love the one who is leading. For didn't his Son say, "This is life eternal, that they might know thee"?

When Jesus showed me that little sister Bee had always longed for, the little girl who would have completed our family and whose death had left an empty place in my heart and in Jacques' that would never be filled, the child I would never hold in my arms down here on earth, but whom I would one day meet in heaven, I realized that in spite of the pain that glimpse had provoked, once again, through her, I was experiencing that unconditional agape love that had been so generously given me throughout my life.

Until that moment I had believed that the dreadful wound was closed. But I now know, so many years afterward, when the vision is still as clear as it was on that April morning, that it was my daughter's sweet, forgiving smile that put the Lord's seal on my final healing.

And it is to her memory that I dedicate this book.